They Left Us Behind

The Story of a Young Girl's Family and the Struggle to Reach America

Jack Freeze and Cungdiem Tang

iUniverse, Inc.
Bloomington

They Left Us Behind

The Story of a Young Girl's Family and the Struggle to Reach America

iUniverse books may be ordered through booksellers or by contacting:

iUniverse
1663 Liberty Drive
Bloomington, IN 47403
www.iuniverse.com
1-800-Authors (1-800-288-4677)

ISBN: 978-1-4502-7357-2 (sc)
ISBN: 978-1-4502-7358-9 (e)
ISBN: 978-1-4502-7359-6 (hc)

Printed in the United States of America

iUniverse rev. date: 1/13/2011

Cover background courtesy of Tuan Tran Photo Galleries

Dedicated to Cungdiem Tang

and her Family

and to all the people that have struggled for

Freedom

CONTENTS

AUTHOR'S NOTE

Cungdiem is the source of her family's history which includes stories and dialogue collected from her parents and family coupled with her own experiences. Jack Freeze created the narrative by combining political events and cultural surroundings with the contents of the diary in a chronological order to give the total perspective of the story.

AUTHOR'S ACKNOWLEDGEMENT

This is a story based on facts presented by members of the family. Any departure from accuracy applies only to some of the dialogue and the descriptions of the surroundings while they were on their journeys. Yet these surroundings were the most likely to be encountered under the circumstances. The conclusions drawn from this narrative and related research are exclusively those of the author.

"The harder the conflict, the more glorious the triumph!" – Thomas Paine

"Never give up!" – Winston Churchill

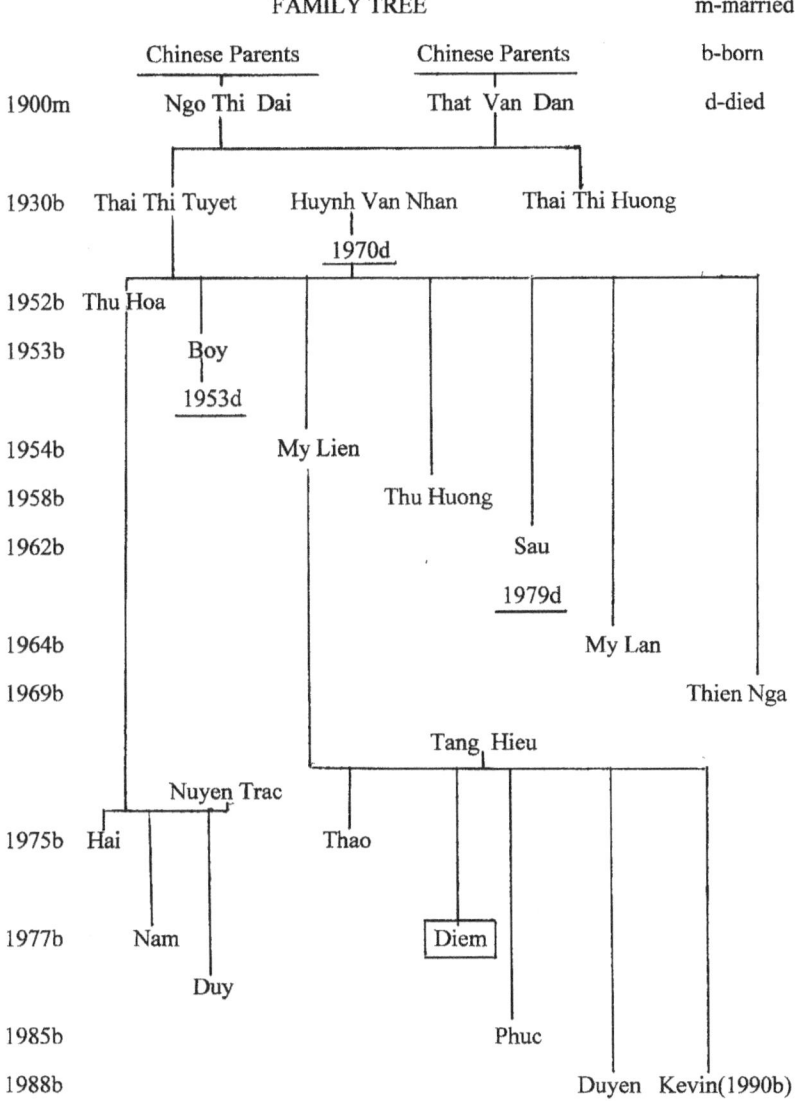

FAMILY TREE   m-married

Chinese Parents   Chinese Parents   b-born

1900m   Ngo Thi Dai   That Van Dan   d-died

1930b   Thai Thi Tuyet   Huynh Van Nhan   Thai Thi Huong
                                1970d

1952b   Thu Hoa

1953b   Boy
                   1953d

1954b   My Lien

1958b   Thu Huong

1962b   Sau
                               1979d

1964b   My Lan

1969b   Thien Nga

                          Tang Hieu
             Nuyen Trac
1975b   Hai   Thao

1977b   Nam   Diem
             Duy

1985b   Phuc

1988b   Duyen   Kevin(1990b)

xi

FOREWORD

An American helicopter hovered over a roof near the United States embassy while terrified South Vietnamese refugees tried to climb aboard from the single file ladder. This fleeting scene would be repeated over and over again on stateside network television. Saigon had fallen. The war was nearly over and the United States had left!

How could the greatest military power on earth not subjugate a small country like North Vietnam? This was the obsessive question that played on the minds of most loyal South Vietnamese, especially the more affluent citizens that could be readily victimized by the conquerors for their transparent wealth and social standing. Yet, on the other hand, the average hard working people could now be terrorized and forced into submission regarding the loss of their homes, their possessions, and even their lives – and indeed, that was the state of affairs!

History records that religion frequently plays a dominant role in the dynamics of international relations. It was certainly true in the case of French-Vietnamese relations. During the 17th century when Vietnam was just beginning to occupy the Mekong Delta, a Jesuit priest by the name of Father Alexandre de Rhodes founded a mission to evangelize the local inhabitants. The next century produced widespread trade between Vietnam and Europe with France becoming heavily involved in Vietnam during the nineteenth century under the guise of protecting the Paris Foreign Missions Society.

But then the Nguyen Dynasty began to see Catholic missionaries as a threat to their political integrity. Attempts were made to expel the missionaries and Napoleon III reacted by sending a fleet with 3,000 soldiers to quell the persecutions and recommence the propagation of the faith. Saigon was then captured in 1859 and the Vietnamese government was forced to cede territories to France.

By 1863, France had established a protectorate over Cambodia and with victory over China in the Sino-French War, French Indochina was established that included Cambodia, all of the territory in modern Vietnam, and eventually Laos. Encroachments were then made on Siam, which led to the transfer of territories back and forth between the two countries. By 1930, the Vietnamese people had had enough. Native soldiers in the French army mutinied in the name of the Vietnamese Nationalist Party. Friction also continued against Siam, now called Thailand, until 1940, resulting in transfers of lands back to Thailand.

World War Two then changed the political scene in France. Germany's occupation resulted in a puppet government called Vichy France and they granted Germany's ally Japan, access to Tonkin province in northern Vietnam where Hanoi was located. This gave Japan a forward base to invade all of Vietnam and to combat the Chinese forces of Chiang Kai-shek in an effort to control the entire Pacific basin. Upon the end of the war and the defeat of Japan, Vietnam once again fell under the influence of France.

The renewed effort to exert hegemony over Indochina would now begin to be challenged. A former French steamship cook who later became trained in Moscow, had emerged on the scene with a new communist movement called Vietminh. His name was Nguyen Tat Thanh, but he was now known as Ho Chi Minh – the "Enlightener". When Japan surrendered, Ho Chi Minh and the Vietminh proclaimed the Democratic Republic of Vietnam in Hanoi, with him as president. But since the French were unwilling to grant independence, war was declared – The First Indochina War!

Immediately, British, French, Indian, and captured Japanese soldiers restored French control. Ho reacted and again declared independence with recognition from China and the Soviet Union. His Vietminh guerillas would then struggle for eight years until they achieved a major victory against the French at a northwest outpost called Dien Bien Phu. Ho Chi Minh had been widely admired for his simplicity, integrity, and determination which played a major role in the development of the Vietnamese strategy for making war. His general at Dien Bien Phu, General Vo Nguyen Giap, implemented tactics based on a closely integrated military and political strategy called "dau tranh". He was inspired by the definitive work of Sun Tzu, a 6th century BC treatise called "The Art Of War".

It had taken 100 years but France was finally forced to leave Vietnam. They could no longer control the colonies so Paris sued for peace. The timing was not favorable for the Vietnamese victors. The cold war between the west and the Soviet Union was exacerbated by the recent Korean conflict and both the Soviet and Chinese communist powers preferred to defer to France by having the Vietnamese delegates partition the country at the 17th parallel - a similar arrangement like the partition of Korea that was successful with a pro-western south. This agreement called the Geneva Peace Accords, would provide for national elections in 1956 to reunite the country.

The United States with its policy of containing communist expansion, countered the agreement with the establishment of SEATO- the Southeast Asia Treaty Organization. It was felt that a reunited Vietnam would come under the control of the communist victors. Under SEATO, the Eisenhower White House created the Government of the Republic of Vietnam in southern Vietnam with an elected president, Ngo Dinh Diem.

Diem soon began to show paranoid tendencies by claiming that North Vietnam was going to overthrow South Vietnam by force and that communists had infiltrated his country. With the help of the American Central Intelligence Agency, thousands of arrests were made and Law 10/59 was passed to confine suspicious people without charges – a suspension of habeas corpus. This was corrupt, and the oppression was protested by the South Vietnamese people including students, professionals, peasants, and religious. The protests culminated in the self-immolation of Buddhist monks after repressive acts were committed against Buddhist monks by the pro-Catholic Diem regime.

There was mixed reaction to Diem on all sides. The Kennedy administration released a report called the "December 1961 White Paper". It recommended an increase in military, technical, and economic aid with advisors to shore up the Diem regime. On the other side, the Communist party made an attempt to cause unrest in the south but the internal southern communists instead demanded a violent overthrow of the Diem government. Consequently, the National Liberation Front was rejuvenated from the days of the French occupation to recruit both communists and non-communists for the effort to unify Vietnam. Anyone could belong as long as they wanted to depose Diem. Washington tried to disparage the purpose of the Front by claiming that Hanoi was trying to create a united communist Vietnam. They labeled the Front with a demeaning title – Viet Cong!

President Kennedy decided to send more equipment and advisors to Vietnam, but not troops. The attempt to isolate villagers from the NLF did not work and the local people were further estranged from Diem. In fact, some of them decided to join the Viet Cong. After the Buddhist incident, some of the South Vietnam generals visited the American Embassy in Saigon with a request to overthrow Diem. As Washington looked the other way, Diem was killed. Three weeks later, John F. Kennedy was assassinated in Dallas, Texas.

Congress then reacted to an attack on American warships and unanimously passed the Gulf Of Tonkin Resolution that gave President Linden Johnson enhanced war powers. After much debate between the Joint Chiefs of Staff and Pentagon civilians over the amount of escalation required, Johnson ordered bombing missions called "Operation Rolling Thunder". Hanoi reacted with a military strategy to get the United States tied down in a winless war, especially now that Johnson had committed the first American combat troops to Vietnam.

The American fear that Vietnam would become the next domino in the communist takeover of Southeast Asia countered the desire for a free market there. It was hoped that Japan would now have markets and that Britain could reestablish their rubber and tin industries in Malaya. In addition, United States credibility was at stake, the South Vietnamese could not be abandoned.

Johnson had every intention to fight a limited war for two reasons, the Chinese would not get involved as they did in Korea, and the North Vietnamese could not outlast American military strength. Yet the heavy bombing had little effect on the rural countryside, the South Vietnamese government was virtually non-existent, and the effort to win the hearts and minds of the peasants was culturally and politically inadequate. On the other hand, United States troops had decisive victories over Viet Cong and the North Vietnamese Army at Chu Lai and the Ia Drang valley. Hanoi learned quickly – do not take on American forces in conventional battles, concentrate on small isolated actions.

The Second Indochina War showed that the communists held the initiative – 88 percent of all engagements were initiated by the Viet Cong and NVA. Basically, actions were avoided unless chances of success were good and fighting was restricted to 1 day in thirty with the remainder of the time spent on population control, training, intelligence gathering, and fortifications. When actions were favorable, the time and places for attacks and defense were carefully considered. After an engagement, units examined their actions through "criticism and self-criticism" sessions with feedback incorporated into future operations.

American reaction was the implementation of the highly successful "search and destroy" tactics including the highly publicized "body counts" along with pacification policies. However, over time, the asylum in Laos and Cambodia permitted the communists to infiltrate more troops from the north and recruit more Viet Cong from the south. As a result, battles would occur in remote regions while civilian interaction would take place in the populated areas. The United States had to match the continuing supply of manpower with a draft of American men.

In January 1968, the combined forces of Viet Cong and North Vietnamese launched the Tet Offensive that included attacks on cities throughout South Vietnam and an assault on the Marines at Khe Sanh. Airlifts to Khe Sanh and a hard fought battle at Hue with the reoccupation of the Citadel and the Imperial Palace by American and South Vietnamese units resulted in heavy losses for the enemy.

But the confidence of the Americans at home was shaken! The draft had been enacted and 58,000 Americans would be killed and 150,000 wounded. President Johnson would not run for reelection and his successor Richard Nixon decided to end the involvement by building up the ARVN army. Pressure had been applied by protests on college campuses and the left wing "Students For A Democratic Society" held massive rallies on the Washington Mall and other places. The country was divided. When Nixon launched heavy bombing raids on Hanoi and the seaport of Haiphong, the international community was outraged. Finally, hostilities were ended between the United States and North Vietnam with the Paris Peace Agreement in January 1973. The South Vietnam Government would have to fight alone for the next two years against the communists until the end came with the capture of the Presidential Palace in Saigon. As a celebration of victory, Saigon would be renamed Ho Chi Minh city.

INTRODUCTION

Some miles below the former South Vietnamese capital was an apprehensive family studiously following events from their home and pondering how these circumstances would affect their future. Would they be accepted as citizens in the communist North Vietnam Government or would their mandarin affiliation with the former democratic government seal their fate? The North Vietnamese Army had rolled into the beloved city along National Highway One with banners flying from their powerful tanks while the Viet Cong insurgents rode along and brandished their weapons.

As the dust settled from the victorious onslaught, the beleaguered family began to watch and wait while they performed devotional services three times a day to bolster their faith in the Pure Land version of Mahayana Buddhism. Through the practice of walking meditation, study of sutras, and the repetitive chanting of "amitabha Budda", they prayed that the purification of their bad karma would free them from worldly desires and place them in a liberated state of enlightenment. This goal of achieving Bodhi would help them cope with the reality of communist occupation. The alternative would be to find a new life in another country and many people would struggle to do just that!

CHAPTER 1

MEKONG DELTA

"The Family"

I was called Cungdiem, and this is my story. It begins with my great grandparents Ngo Thi Dai and That Van San. They were united through an arranged marriage by their Chinese parents, recent immigrants from China. A small farming village called Phu Loc in southern Vietnam was where they settled around the year 1900.

The village was ideally located in the rich farmland of the Mekong Delta where the Mekong River enters after meandering for 2800 miles from the plateau of Tibet. Upon reaching the delta, this River of Nine Dragons splits into numerous branches that spread throughout the region. Phu Loc is twelve miles from the South China Sea as the crow flies, and it lies along National Highway One between the towns of Bac Lieu and Soc Trang in the Soc Trang province. Saigon could be reached along this highway by traveling around 150 miles to the north.

My great grandparents brought their Chinese culture with them as they easily settled into the small town of two hundred residents, mostly of Chinese descent. Fortunately for us, we can now claim to be bilingual, having the ability to speak Cantonese as well as Vietnamese – not counting English of course. People will argue though whether Cantonese is a unique language or a dialect of the Chinese language. I think it can be viewed in two ways; it is either a dialect for ethnic and cultural reasons or a separate language because it is unintelligible with other variations of Chinese. Oh well, the main thing was that we could understand just about everybody that came along.

Aside from the ethnic connections to the townspeople, the area was an abundant "rice bucket" and "fruit bucket" with coconut, longan, and mango trees, thanks to the waterways that provided the nourishing silt from neighboring countries to enrich the soil. Of course, they had their foreign occupations, every country wanted this bountiful land.

The French especially! It wasn't fair! Just before my grandparents arrived, French Indochina was established in 1887 with Cambodia and three Vietnamese regions; Tonkin in the north, Annam in the central region, and Cochinchina in the south. Laos was added in 1893. Two years after they arrived, the capital was moved from Saigon to Hanoi. The country was in turmoil. Even though the monarchy was preserved, they were only figureheads. French authority would control and implement the policies under this façade. And to add insult to injury, all of the provinces except Cochinchina would be French protectorates. Cochinchina would be ruled directly.

My great grandparents had to be wary when protecting their culture. France was imposing a policy of adoption rather than relying on one of association where native rulers could keep their culture and hierarchy while making policy. The French Revolution principles of equality, liberty, and fraternity, would now be applied to the colonies. So Indochina would be "Frenchized" with French as the official language of the government. The Indochinese were going to be turned into Frenchmen!

Resentment throughout the country resulted from the conflicting values and customs of the French as compared to the traditions of the Indochinese. Small towns like Phu Loc depended on the tradition of group problem solving and decision making. It was not easy for my grandparents to not be involved in local politics as the wave of French individualism swept in to local governments. French influence was having a devastating effect on local society and it was a bitter pill to swallow for the newly arrived immigrants.

INDOCHINA

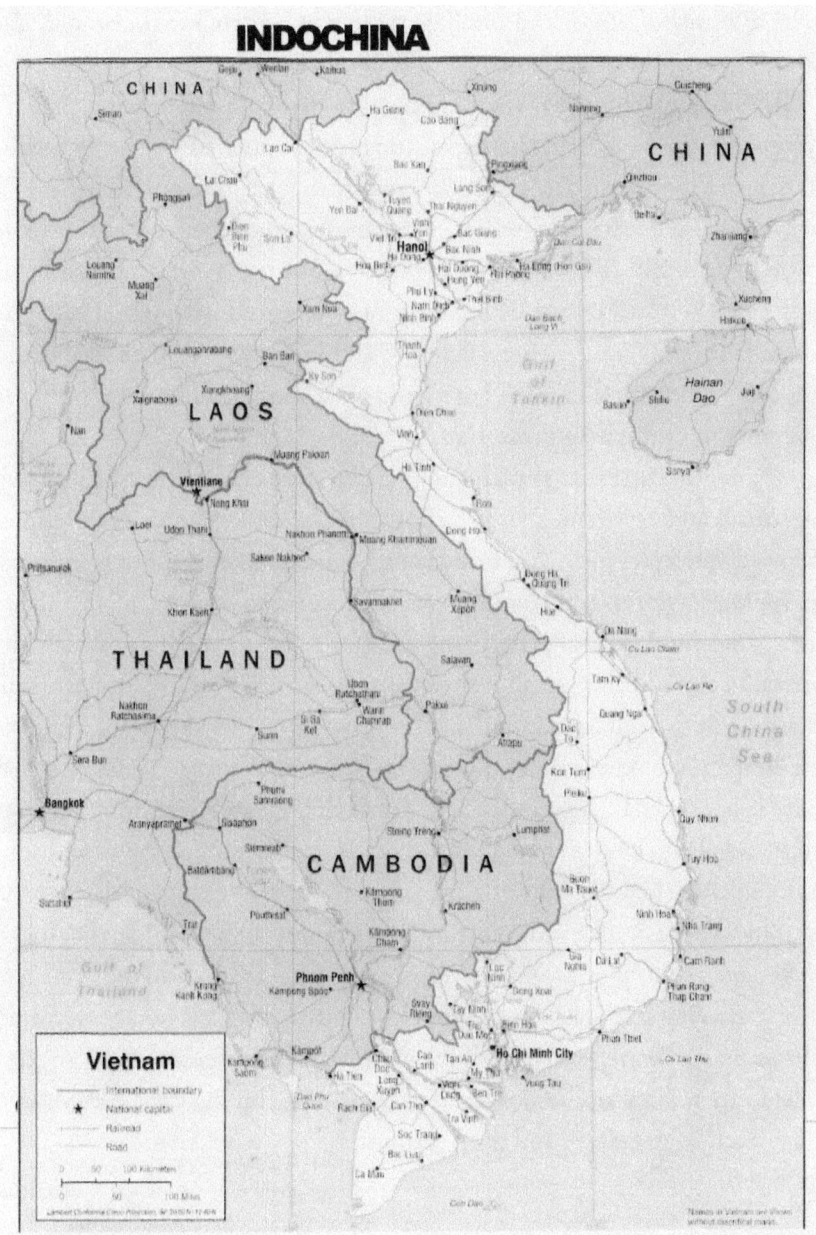

Courtesy of the University of Texas Libraries, The University of Texas at Austin

But life goes on! In the summer of 1930, they were blessed with the first of two daughters and they named her Thai Thi Tuyet. She would grow up to be a beautiful, kind, and intelligent woman. Of course she would, she would become my grandmother!

In spite of the Vietnamese mutinies in the French army, Japan's occupation during World War Two, and now the guerilla war being fought by the Vietminh, my great grandparents managed to live a fairly normal farming life and were able to provide for my grandmother's education. The tuition costs, difficult entry requirements, and transportation problems to the nearby town of Soc Trang were overcome and Thai Thi Tuyet was entered into college there in the fall of 1951. Her major would be the French language which would enable her to find work more readily, perhaps in the government or teaching profession.

Our young first year student adapted well into college life. She was well organized and disciplined so her class attendance and homework studies followed a strict regimen. But being young with a great love for the outdoors, an appreciation learned from her parents, she would venture out during her spare time for long walks along the trails and canals that divided the emerald colored fields. In the more dense areas, the thick palm groves on each side of the canals would almost overlap to form a canopy of shade as the sampans would be rowed along underneath by a lone farmer as he stood there in his Ao ba ba and conical hat. These clothes were very functional for work and play. The silk shirt was long sleeved and buttoned down and split at the sides at the waist, making two flaps. In front were two pockets at the bottom – very popular and colorful! At other times, she would pass groups of women bending over and harvesting rice in a paddy field while others were gathering rice stalks into piles. When they noticed her, they would all rise up and wave with a friendly greeting. The ravages of the incessant hillside guerrilla war had not reached these unassuming people even with the French colonization and the Vietminh.

SOC TRANG

Courtesy of Wikimedia Commons under the GNU Free Documentation License

PAGODAS

The first semester had been easy for grandmother. She already knew the basics of her courses from her rigorous training at home and the local school. But spring time had arrived and April would bring the blossoms and bird migrations. Her walks would now include a search for the popular Asian Koel, a member of the cuckoo family of birds. They would be easy to spot being 18 inches long with a long tail. The male is blue-black with a red eye while the female is dark brown with white streaks across the body. Grandmother would quietly listen for the melodious song of the male, a repeated "Koo-Ooo" during the breeding season while the female would respond with a shrill "kik-kik-kik". Her favorite bird was the red-headed crane with nearly a six foot wing span. These birds were almost friendly, sometimes landing on the sampans several at a time. The skies would also be darkened at times with the huge flocks of nearly 800 species of birds seeking sanctuary from the northern winters.

She always insisted though, that her most enjoyable excursions during that time of year were her visits to the Hoa Phuong trees to enjoy the flamboyant blossoms that were now thick on the branches. They represented the many happy and sad school memories of the past year. So, in Vietnam, the flower is also known as "hoa hoc tro" or the student's flower and it blossoms just at the end of the school year as a signal to enjoy the days of summer.

While standing before the bright orange and red blossoms one day during her final semester before graduation, she noticed someone walking along the path toward her.

"Chao ba Co," he cheerfully said as he waved

"And hello to you too," she smiled.

"May I share the beauty of your view?" he continued while approaching her. My, how elegant she thought as she noticed the handsome features of the young man. She had seen him on campus so she was not concerned about having a pleasant conversation. In fact, she intended to enjoy it.

"Oh yes, the beauty of the flame tree belongs to everyone. Come join me."

He then slowly bowed his head and said, "My name is Huynh Van Nhan."

"And I am Thai Thi Tuyet from Phu Loc," she replied.

6

They would meet many times near these trees and discuss their studies, their families and their future. And the relationship had become serious by the time the school semester had ended. But graduation would end their ability to visit each other, so Nhan expressed his love for her and proposed marriage.

This turn of events was quite a shock to the Thai family. They resented the fact that she might marry and move away immediately after graduation. They had hoped that she would help support the family with a decent income now that she had an education.

The Vietnamese custom of a marriage proposal required that the man should take his parents to the home of the girl's family and make a formal proposal. So Nhan, being the gentleman that he was, arranged for his family to meet the Thais. The young bride to be was very nervous when the Huynh family arrived in Phu Loc. Would she be embarrassed or would her family be unfriendly? She need not have worried and perhaps she should have given more credit to her parents.

They welcomed the visitors who were well known as a proper and prosperous family. The marriage was arranged and Tuyet would now be known as Huynh Thai Thi Tuyet, and happily so.

A short two years later, my grandmother decided to apply for a teaching position at a local school in Phu Loc. She was accepted and began to teach during the day while trying to help her husband develop a restaurant business in the evenings. In addition, they considered opening a billiard bar. But more importantly, their main concern, and in fact their dream, was to have a family. Now would be a good a time as any. Most of the small villages throughout the countryside were controlled by the Vietminh guerrillas and the people wanted independence. They had been slaves of the Chinese for a thousand years and were now slaves of the French, you might as well say that, for a hundred years.

To sustain local support, the Vietminh Youth league consisting of organized teenagers, would travel the regions and teach the populace about patriotism and independence. Communism was not discussed, only the rich heritage of Vietnam and the strength of the people.

Besides, the center of the revolution in the Mekong Delta was hundreds of miles to the north at Ben Tre although occasionally Vietminh guerrillas could be seen walking by Phu Loc. There was a pride about them and they wore their rolled up straw mats across their backs as badges of identification. Sometimes while passing a village they would sing the "Mat Song of the Resistance"!

The war was concentrated around the larger towns where French blockhouses would be attacked by the Vietminh. Then the French would retaliate by raiding villages along the coast to destroy everything in their path. Artillery would be used along with planes that would bomb and strafe the people. Survivors would then flee to the mountains.

Stories would be told by friends farther north about bodies lying everywhere after a raid. One girl had been burned by napalm and all that the villagers could do was gather around the dying youth at night while her body glowed with phosphorus in the darkness.

How could my grandparents maintain a normal family life with the country in such turmoil? It must have taken strength and faith to endure. Yet in the Spring of 1952, they welcomed their first born, a girl named Thu Hoa. Since Vietnamese culture put family pressure on having a boy, the next year they had another baby and it was a boy. Oh how they celebrated! Nearly the entire town joined the party.

One could tell the background or affiliation of the guests by the clothes that they wore. Some of the people employed by the French were wearing European suits and dresses along with the university students. Other folks, mainly the revolutionary or Vietminh supporters, expressed their allegiance in black. But most of the rural guests remained faithful to their national dress and wore simple pajama-type shirts and trousers – a kind of silent opposition to French colonialism. They consisted of a snug collar while buttoned down on the left side to the waist. The female dress would flow from a tight waist down to the heels while the male clothes only extended to the knees. Blue was the popular color. The younger women wore an Ao Yem, a square cut piece of cloth over the front tied with strings at the neck and back. Red and Pink were popular for festive occasions such as this. The whole affair was a kaleidoscope of colors.

The ever popular Nem was served which consisted of pork, pig skin, fresh sliced garlic, and black pepper in grape or banana leaves. Other dishes of heavy amounts of rice, herbs, and vegetables were served with a minimum of oil and meat and that was used only as a seasoning – a most healthy and delicious meal. Especially after having consistent daily portions of noodle soup with vegetables and fish sauce eaten out of your personal "Pho" or bowl. For dessert, tea was served with O Mai, a dried apricot along with Banh Khui, the traditional cake made of a rice ball flavored with green bean paste, pork, and spices, all on a plate of cabbage leaves or cudwood leaves found along the edges of the rice fields.

Politics and insurgency were soon forgotten as the revelers enjoyed the merrymaking and attention shown to the new infant boy. Music complemented the feast with sweet, soft, haunting Vietnamese melodies. They floated along like a gentle breeze caressing the flowers of a tree in springtime. One could imagine the slow moving blossoms swaying back and forth with the rhythm of the music that blends so well with the sweet and gentle nature of the people. The young family was so happy, they had a girl and a boy which made the grandparents quite satisfied. The family name would flourish! But it was not to be. One month later, the infant contracted an unknown disease and perished. Grandmother Tuyet was devastated!

Not only was she sad over the loss of her child, but the cultural pressure by the husband's family for a male child to carry on the name could result in their desire for Nhan to remarry if Tuyet could not have a male heir. And medical tradition at that time placed the blame on the woman regardless of the husband's health.

Tuyet was not to be discouraged! She loved Nhan very much and wanted to please him and his family if it took several pregnancies. Yet, in the back of her mind she knew that he could remarry without her consent and bring the woman into the same household while she remained there. So they began to plan for another child in the Fall of 1953 knowing that Tuyet could still help to support the family by teaching French. Especially since the French Army commander, General Henri Navarre had now created a permanent base at Dienbienphu in spite of the loss of popularity for the war back home.

April 1954 arrived and the family was blessed with another girl. They named her My Lien while Nhan became more desperate for a boy. The women all fawned over her and were quite taken with her dark complexion and cute little button nose. Meanwhile the in-laws continued to put pressure on Tuyet and she agreed to keep trying even with the business demands and household chores. However, she was no longer sure about teaching French. Since March, General Vo Nguyen Giap and the Vietnamese Army had surrounded the French Army at Dienbienphu with the last position falling on May 7, one month after the birth of My Lien. The family now wondered about how much of a culture shock the country would experience.

The very next day, May 8, the Geneva Convention opened and France with an unpopular war on its hands, agreed to full independence for the northern half of the country under the Vietminh leadership of Ho Chi Minh. These Geneva Accords also guaranteed that a nationwide election would be held in two years for the purpose of reunification.

By July, most of the Vietminh forces had left the South and regrouped in the North above the 17th parallel. The French and their Vietnamese compatriots would move southward. The Accords also allowed for civilians to cross the line and one million North Vietnamese migrated to the South. These included Buddhist monks, Catholic citizens, and anti-communists since the Moscow trained Ho Chi Minh would now impose the Communist movement on the northern people.

So both North and South Vietnam would experience a culture shock. In the North, the totalitarian Communist government would impose harsh restrictions and demands on the people. In the South, the Buddhist religion would be revitalized and the Catholic influence would become noticeable.

The United States became concerned that the reunification of the country would result in a Communist state. Having won the war against France, Ho Chi Minh was the power in the country, a fait accompli! So the Southeast Asia Treaty Organization (SEATO) was created and with American aid the Government of the Republic of Vietnam (GVN) was established in South Vietnam with the Catholic Ngo Dinh Diem as president. It would be a harsh regime as the paranoid president felt that the northern Communists were infiltrating his country. He began to arrest thousands, especially some of the former Vietminh, with Buddhists, students, and peasants beginning to protest in the streets.

How did this upheaval affect the folks at Phu Loc? The Vietminh were not active there and the new Democratic government at Saigon seemed to not bother the local citizens in the outlying districts . Nhan and Tuyet could feel at ease for awhile and continue to grow the restaurant business and strive for a boy. She could even continue to teach French because of the strong French influence in the demographics of the people – French restaurants and architecture in Vietnam, educations in Paris, and many ex-patriates now living in France.

In spite of the corrupt rule of Diem, the young family enjoyed relative quiet while welcoming yet another daughter to the household in 1958. Her name would be Thu Huong and she was very different from her sisters with light skin and Oriental shaped eyes. Now with three daughters and a business to run , Nhan decided to hire a housekeeper to help Tuyet while he commuted to Bac Lieu, a small town about fifteen miles south of Phu Loc, noted for its bird sanctuary. He had been hired to help the local people learn how to read French.

Since they were now enjoying a modest affluence, helped in part by the influx of citizens from the North, Nhan would occasionally bring along food and clothing to the poor peasants in Bac Lieu, a quiet gesture on his part that endeared him to the people.

With both Nhan and Tuyet having been well educated, they followed the political events with great interest. Especially now that men were beginning to disappear from the villages. The government was arresting former Vietminh guerrillas with charges of subversion since their allegiance had been with Ho Chi Minh.

One evening while Nhan was showing the children how to make toys with bamboo, paper and coconut leaves, Tuyet suggested that they take the children to Bac Lieu on his next visit to show them the bird sanctuary. "I would like to go but I worry about your traveling there with all the suspicion and arrests being made," she wondered.

"Oh we'll be safe, if we're stopped for questioning, just pretend to be a loyal Diem citizen as long as they hold the whip," he answered.

"But I don't like the way they treat people differently and unfairly, especially if they are not Catholic," she continued.

"Listen, I know there's a double standard in the country, what with great buildings, cars, and wealth in the cities surrounded by shanties, street people and prostitutes. As long as we keep an inner allegiance to ourselves about family, work, and our faith in Ong Ba", he added, "we'll be loyal to our principles."

"Yes, I agree," she responded, "but our Ong Ba religion is mainly about ancestor worship and not the formal Buddhist faith as practiced by the monks, so we're caught in the middle, monks protesting and Catholics getting all the privileges."

"Well, you know Diem's brother, Ngo Dinh Nhu is the security chief. He's the one who is holding the arrested people in jail without bringing charges. The problem is that the more the Buddhist monks, students, and business people demonstrate, the louder Diem gets about the Communists taking the South by force," Nhan insisted.

"Don't forget that Diem's brother is also Bishop of Vinh Lang. Together they're using government money to build Catholic churches in the countryside. People professing to be Catholic are getting rice, clothes, and even corrugated tin for their roofs while the Buddhists and others are getting nothing. Some folks are even converting to become Catholic just for the handouts. Where do you think all of this turmoil will end?" Tuyet sighed.

"There's either going to be a civil war in the South between Diem's Catholic government and the combined Buddhists and northern sympathizers that want reunification or a war against North Vietnam and their insurgents in the South."

Tuyet looked at her husband and saw in his eyes a prophetic air of resignation as he sadly glanced at the children and wondered about the future.

In spite of the political upheaval, Nhan was not about to give up on his quest for a male heir. He complains to Tuyet that he is sick and tired of his family that relentlessly reminds him of the responsibility to preserve the Huynh family name. Yet he is also constantly being reminded of the civil strife in South Vietnam by the never ending neighborhood gossip about the latest arrests and protests in the streets of Saigon. The latest rumor is that guerrilla organizations are rebuilding in the south and that North Vietnam has started to infiltrate men and material down a series of roads called the Ho Chi Minh Trail!

His decision to have more children was made after much soul searching over the risks facing their future and the desire to maintain some semblance of a peaceful family life. The decision was finalized when Tuyet gave birth in the late summer of 1962 to a beautiful, fair skinned infant, with long black hair. They named the child Sau – it was another girl!

By all appearances, it was a peaceful family life. On his days at home after the work week, Nhan would play with the four girls and show great love. They would cling to his arms and sit high on his shoulders as he marched around the room while Tuyet would complain about the need to be careful –to no avail of course. He had no favorites which pleased Tuyet and she continued to bless him with tender loving care as they pursued the quest for that male child.

One would think that they had paid their allegiance to his family, at least with the effort. Nhan certainly thought so and he showed his appreciation to Tuyet for trying to please his family by small displays of affection, little things like placing a flower in her hair after carefully bringing it home from work. She would teasingly respond and then ask why would he give her so much attention.

"Because your smile brings me so much peace and happiness," he lovingly responded. "And when I place the flower in your hair, I see that smile."

It was remarkable that they could live in such surroundings, joyfully raising the family while struggling to teach and run the business. They seemed to live in a vacuum, isolated from the troubled world that they occupied. The rejuvenated guerrilla movement in the south was now officially under the auspices of the North Vietnamese Communist Party and it was called the National Liberation Front. It served to provide organization for all of the opposition movements toward Diem. Anyone could join the united front as long as they opposed Diem and violence would be the order of the day.

The fortified guerrillas controlled the southern half of the Mekong Delta while the northern half was still being contested. Thirty-eight thousand troops of Diem's government faced 15,000 guerrillas in the upper part of the Delta. If control there was lost, the South Vietnam Government would not survive and the United States decided to react by sending military advisors, equipment, and more aid to the Saigon government. Full scale war broke out and the United States, in spite of the claim that the National Liberation Front was independent of the Hanoi Communists, labeled the NLF with a demeaning term that meant Vietnamese Communist. They called it the "Viet Cong"!

Getting to Bac Lieu was no longer a question of being fearful of the Diem government, it was considerably worse. To be arrested on suspicion of subverting the Saigon government was one thing but now the Viet Cong were making the secondary roads impassable to vehicles by having the peasants dig ditches across them and dismantle the bridges. The lower Delta especially, saw the road beds being dug up with the dirt scattered across the rice paddies. And the Saigon government did not have the cooperation of the local people to suppress the guerrilla insurgents. The destruction of the road beds was intended to slow down the South Vietnam patrols but it also hampered the civilians that had to commute for work. Nhan would have to circumvent the roads if traveling by car or hitch rides in carts that could go off road when necessary. There was also the nagging fear that the South Vietnam army patrol would contact a hidden Viet Cong group and engage in a firefight or there could be an ambush set up as Nhan went through. It had to be extremely stressful for him and the other folks, mainly the professional people.

It seems like difficult times brings out the best in people. That was certainly true of my grandparents and the girls. They would continue to celebrate the holidays during the next few years in spite of the civil unrest and threats from the north.

For instance, January of 1963 would see them celebrate the New Year by providing new clothing for the family. Three outfits for each member were made or purchased to be worn on the three days before New Year's day, actually. The usual household chores were avoided during this time while the family visited with neighbors and friends who had also prepared for the celebration. In addition, cash had been saved to be placed in brightly colored red envelopes for gifts to the children. On the first morning, the children would bring tea and cakes to the family as a token of respect and good will. Then they would wish for each member to have a New Year that would be the best ever, and to also live a long, healthy, and prosperous life while they stayed young forever.

As the adults and older relatives enjoyed their treat, they would also express the same sentiment to the children while giving them the red envelopes with hao or dong coins in them. Most families preferred the Vietnamese dong over the French Indochina piaster, which was still in circulation.

Food was then gathered for the tables that had been cooked over several days prior to the feast days while the children met their friends to play Bau Cua Ca Cop, a card game that gambles with the money. This New Year food called Banh tet consists of sweet rice, mung beans, coconut, and pork that had been steamed in banana leaves for eight hours and then drained. Enough food had been prepared to last the three days. For dessert, dried fruit and candy called Muc is served with Hat Dua, the popular watermelon seed, all considered as traditional food for the New Year.

Once the food was complete, all necessary cleaning was finished, again prior to the three day celebration, else the superstition that all your wealth will be swept away may come to be true. This fear is so strong that other families would not permit a visit by people who violate the tradition, it would bring bad luck to them as well!

To counter the success of the National Liberation Front throughout the countryside, via the Viet Cong, Washington and Diem's Saigon regime decided to put in place a counterinsurgency plan called the "Strategic Hamlet Program". The intent was to isolate the Viet Cong from their base of support, namely the local villagers. So these local people began to be rounded up and relocated some distance to "safe hamlets" that were built by the Diem government. This removal of people from their homes and neighborhoods had a disastrous affect. The remoteness of the Saigon government had now reached the countryside which created ill feeling toward the government, so much so that more recruits were signing up for the Viet Cong. Nhan and his family were still secure in their home; they were well established in the community through their teaching professions and restaurant and they carefully maintained a neutral non-political appearance. But there were some families in the area that were subject to relocation mainly those with former Vietminh connections.

Even though the Vietnamese people were a combination of different political, social, and ethnic groups, they all suffered the disillusion and psychological trauma brought on mainly by the current state of the country. But there was still an idealism and courageous characteristic about them that gave them the will to hold on. " Hold on" was the byword, all things will pass and the people, in spite of the controlling factions, will persevere!

And it was evident in the way that they continued to celebrate their holidays. After the celebration of New Year, the end of January brought the Full Moon festival called Ram thang gien. It was a tribute by the farmers for the help received from their God during the harvesting of rice. The Full Moon indicates the completion of a full year of travel of the planets, moon, and sun around the zodiac circle of constellations and ending in the period of Aquarius – an important source of information for the timely planting and harvesting of rice.

Celebrations would be in order, especially after a good yield. People would gather from different cities to perform an opera called Hat Boi. It was always a great program that lasted for three nights especially for the young people to have an excuse to date. The music would be combined with vendor displays of foods, flowers, gifts, and toys. Especially exciting was the opera being sung in Cantonese; it created a kindred feeling as if it were dedicated to our people.

February would see the continuation of the celebration to give thanks for the successful harvesting of other crops as well. This time the opera was called Hat Dinh and it was sung in Vietnamese.

Not to be forgotten were the family members who had passed on to their reward. In March, Thanh Minh day would unite all family members from near and far to have a memorial for the deceased. Visits to the cemetery would be made to respectfully maintain and replenish the area. If folks would gather for a funeral, preparations were considerably different from western societies. The body would be mummified with tea leaves and wrapped in silk. For three days, people would make their visits while monks would pray all day and night in order to free the soul. After that, burial would take place six feet down with the monument three feet above ground. For folks that could afford to pay, a concrete base would be placed over the grave for the monument. It was worth the expense since the tropical weather with the numerous rains would cause the monument to have to be raised and reset each year.

But April is the most beautiful month for weather with low humidity and little rain and it would usher in new life with weddings and receptions.

May is the month for planting and since rice is the most vital cash crop and primary food of the people, many prayers are offered to Than Nong, the God of agriculture, and Than Lua, the God of rice plants, as well as ancestors to protect the farms and fields. The Mekong Delta produces the most rice in Vietnam, and this industry employs nearly 80 percent of the population. This hard manual labor results in Vietnam being the world's third largest exporter of rice. The local farmers near Phu Loc would by now have germinated the rice seeds into shoots a few inches long for planting into the paddy fields – flooded parcels of rich delta soil.

These fields are best served when adjacent to rivers, canals, or marshes that can provide the necessary irrigation. Planting is done by the farmers and their families by wading into the fields that are nearly knee deep in water. Woven baskets or two handed buckets are used to transfer water to the fields. Since typhoons may occur from May to January in the Mekong Delta, May is the best time for planting to take advantage of the extensive flooding.

Vietnamese literature describes a rice field as wide enough for a flock of storks to span their wings across. And the sway of rice plants in the wind is compared to waves of the sea and it is called "song lua".

Only one animal is capable of plowing the paddy fields and that is the water buffalo. They are so important that they are treated like pets and live in a shed next to the family house. They are very gentle and the children play with them and ride their backs. When working, they perform like horses pulling a plow. They are given names and they act protective of the family around strangers. Very important asset!

I speak of this in some detail because most of the people that lived around my grandparents were farmers and this was their lifestyle. Fortunately my grandparents were educated and they could provide services to their neighbors rather than work in the fields like the struggling peasants.

RICE FIELDS

Courtesy of Wikimedia Commons under the GNU Documentation License

However, in May of 1963, events heightened in South Vietnam with not only the Viet Cong activity but also the conflict between the Diem government and militant Buddhists which resulted in demonstrations turning into street clashes. By June, the Saigon government was ready to collapse. Diem's brother had raided the Buddhist pagodas in South Vietnam on charges that they were harboring Communists. Massive protests now took place on the streets of Saigon.

Tuyet's main concern though was the safety of the children that were now on summer vacation. Their age ranged from one to eleven, so it wouldn't take much effort to keep them occupied, especially when the rains let them play in the mud and water.

Nhan would help to care for the children when he was not at work. He would take the nine and eleven year old children, My Lien and Thu Hoa, to the river for them to fish and swim while Tuyet kept the other children at home. One day while they were getting ready to walk to the river, Nhan was startled by the newspaper that had just arrived.

"Tuyet, don't let the children see the newspaper! It is horrible!" he urged. The front page picture showed a Buddhist monk sitting in the middle of the street in Saigon burning to death. He had protested the treatment of the monks with self-immolation. A sacrifice that would be repeated again.

Summer seemed to pass quickly that year for them. July and August were busy times; first the celebration of Thi Vang, where morning prayers to God and ancestors would be followed by families placing rice, cake, and candy outside to be collected and brought to the temple. By afternoon the village leaders would climb to the top of the temple with bunches of wooden sticks labeled with the items and price tags. The people below would line up in their costumes and try to catch the sticks as they were thrown down from above. Later, the fortunate folks would exchange the sticks for the item and pay the fee.

The second event in August involved another Full Moon festival dedicated to the excited children. Full moon cake and candies were distributed followed by a parade with colored lanterns made up of dragons, butterflies, and tigers. The moon cakes came in three varieties all shaped in the form of a small pumpkin. Inside these rich tasting foods are combinations of lotus seeds, ground beans, orange peels, egg, fried onions, peanut and lemon leaves all arranged to have a white or brown color. This Mid-Autumn affair occurs on the most picturesque night of the year as the lanterns are suspended in the air while the costumed children lion dancers perform on the streets. It is one of the most important events in Vietnam with the purpose of promoting education, poetry, dance, arts, and crafts.

For the young men, it is an opportunity to visit the temple and present a written prayer to the monk for his blessing that they will marry a beautiful lady. They then throw the papers into a huge tree, if they don't fall down, the request will come true. The ladies will place a wish in a paper boat or lotus and float it down the river. The farther it sails before sinking, the better their chance of finding love and marriage.

September comes too fast for the children. School begins along with harvest time. Everyone is back to work. Men and women stand bent over in the fields all day with hand sickles. Afterward, the collected sheaves are threshed to remove the rice which is then laid out on mats to dry in the sun. Transportation to market by water is the most efficient means of travel. Huge mounds of rice are loaded onto a flat low sided barge that usually has an ornamental figure on the bow such as a dragon head. In addition to the rice as a main staple, edible rice wrappers called "banh trang" are made from rice flour and water to serve as sandwich wrappers.

The year winds down, October has its rain, November is quiet, and December starts the New Year preparation. But this November 1963 is historic. Ngo Dinh Diem is overthrown and murdered in a military coup.

Another year rolls by and another daughter arrives in the fall of 1964, a dimpled dark skinned angel named My Lan, to bring the total to five. Soon after, the people become shocked when United States bombers start to attack North Vietnam and Marines land in South Vietnam at Da Nang. By 1968, half a million Americans have been invested. A second military coup in Saigon ended with a military regime. From 1966 to 1968, North Vietnamese Army (NVA) groups infiltrate the south through the Ho Chi Minh trail. After several conventional battle victories by the United States, the NVA and Viet Cong resort to a strategy of guerrilla warfare and attrition of the enemy forces along with civilian propaganda. Finally on January 31, 1968, the Tet offensive begins with Viet Cong and NVA

FULL MOON (MID-AUTUMN) FESTIVAL

Mooncakes are often eaten during the festival.

Courtesy of Wikimedia Commons by author Viethavvh

units attacking all the major cities and towns in the country. Unfortunately for them, civilian uprisings did not occur as expected. People like Nhan and other middle class folks realized that in spite of the terrible current government, the Communist forces would create a totalitarian regime and persecute people like Nhan that were perceived to be Saigon supporters.

The offensive resulted in the loss of fifty percent of the Viet Cong manpower effectively neutralizing the southern guerrillas. But President Nixon in May of 1969 started to withdraw the American units in order to turn the war over to the South Vietnam Army. So the loss of the Tet offensive by the north is offset by the upcoming departure of the Americans. The North Vietnamese will regroup, rebuild and return to the war against the weakened South Vietnamese forces.

By fall of 1969 the sixth girl is born, Thien Nga, a plain child that will grow to be a victim of tease by her sisters. This finishes it for Nhan and Tuyet! The quest for a boy child is over!

Sometimes the rainy season seemed to never end, especially this year 1970. It could seem relentless, day in and day out, pouring steady and heavy, bringing everything to a halt. Maybe that was why Tuyet was feeling sad, slightly depressed. One of those occasions where you feel obsessed with the gloom of the weather.

She had been teaching mathematics but kept losing her concentration, making minor but obvious mistakes on the blackboard. Maybe a short break will snap me out of it, I feel kind of run down, she thought. She began to relax in the teacher's lounge when she started to hear a lot of commotion in the hall. Her name was being called out and then the students entered the lounge and came to an abrupt halt. Their eyes were downcast and she asked them to return to the classroom. But with tears glistening on his cheek, one of the students said, "They found your dead husband's body floating in the river down by the market!"

Tuyet dropped her teacup and collapsed to the floor. A dry sob escaped her lips, her breath was frozen, and she seemed to be out of her body, struggling to avoid the reality of those words. Finally she regained control and ran through the steady downpour until her beautiful white Ao Dai was soaked and her well groomed hair was drenched. Upon reaching the market

AO DAI DRESS

Courtesy of Wikimedia Commons by author Peter Kauffner

she pushed her way through the crowd until they made a path for her. His body was still lying in the cold rain and his clothes were torn but there was no blood. She gently touched him and his nose started to bleed profusely, bright, red, and thick. The shock caused her to faint and some people carried her inside to help her recover while other bystanders carried his body to the house. The children found out through their classmates and ran home.

The next day she sat on her front step and dreamed of their yesterdays. Her mind traveled back to the pleasant meetings with Nhan under the Hoa Phuong trees with their beautiful flaming blossoms. She could almost smell the fragrance again. As if speaking to someone, perhaps her husband, she said out loud that she did not understand,

"toi khong hieu!"

" I am alone with six daughters, what am I going to do?"

———————————

———————————

HOA PHUONG TREE

Courtesy of Tuan Tran Photo Galleries

CHAPTER 2

PHU LOC

"An Arranged Marriage"

There is an ancient Buddha quotation that I believe must have been in the forefront of grandmother's thoughts. "The whole secret of existence is to have no fear. Never fear what will become of you, depend on no one. Only the moment you reject all help are you freed!"

Tuyet was determined to move on and raise the family. The poison of vengeance will not smother the love I have for my daughters. My love will keep no record of wrongs, it cannot be any different, Nhan would expect that!

Although she was going to pick herself up and struggle onward, she first had to prepare for the funeral of her beloved husband. So she called the children and had them respectfully gathered around his body as they began the process of covering it with tea leaves. They could hear the steady sound of the neighbor's hammer as he constructed the wooden coffin. They completed the preparation with a linen body cloth and placed the body in the coffin. A prayer paper was then placed under the coffin and burned. This ritual would last for three days as neighbors helped to prepare food for the visitors and friends who came to help. Tuyet would be seen quietly sitting next to the bier while refusing to eat, just taking water and tea. Her

27

emotions would range from one extreme to another, occasional tears then laughter with soft whispering from time to time.

On the third day, some Buddhists monks came to pay their respects and offer prayers before the coffin while neighboring people dug the grave at the cemetery. The children were not allowed to follow the procession to the cemetery because of a Vietnamese phobia. It was believed that once the coffin reaches ground level as it is lowered, the soul of the child could be trapped with the soul of the departed if the child's shadow would fall across the coffin.

As the entourage slowly departed from the cemetery, Tuyet made her way back to the house and sat down once again on the front step to ponder about the cause of Nhan's death. Questions had obsessed her mind for the past four days. Did Nhan have enemies? Why would someone hate him so much that it would lead to murder?

That very afternoon a middle aged man approached Tuyet. He was disheveled looking, wearing dirty and worn clothing with a very large wide brimmed slouch hat. Thinking that he was a beggar, she entered the house and returned with food and water. He thankfully took the offered refreshments then said that he had come to talk to her. While refusing to give his name, he did say that he saw what happened that day near the market and thought that she should be informed.

He said that Nhan was driving a five- wheeled truck that carried seven passengers. They seemed to be relaxed and talking as the truck came by. But suddenly there was a horrendous noise from an explosion that covered the truck with flame and smoke. The passengers were killed outright with some of their bodies torn apart. Nhan's body was ejected from the cab and blown into the river. It must have been a time bomb placed under the truck, he added.

The shock of the revelation was too much for Tuyet. She wept openly until her eyes were nearly closed from the strain. Finally she composed herself and asked, "Do you know who placed the bomb?"

"It was the Communists," he quickly responded.

"But why would they do that to him? He was just a professor and business man who harmed no one, he helped people."

BUDDHIST MONK

Courtesy of Wikimedia Commons by author Jean-Marie Hullot

"Because he helped people, the Communists thought that he was helping the Americans. So they had to kill him."

Even though talks between Secretary of State Kissinger and North Vietnamese politburo member Le Duc Tho were being held in Paris, they were being held in secret so the armies in the field had no knowledge of negotiations. Americans were still destroying bases and supply lines as far away as Cambodia. The Tet Offensive loss was still bitter in the eyes of the Viet Cong and NVA. These "bo dai" soldiers would not hesitate to eliminate any person who was suspect of supporting American or South Vietnam activities.

Because of his affluence and status as a teaching professor, Nhan appeared to be a tacit supporter of the Saigon government in the eyes of the insurgents. He tried his best to remain uninvolved but the killing of a prominent person under the guise of being patriotic would promote the stature of a Viet Cong recruit. And ironically, all Vietnamese understood the intervention of a colonial power such as the Chinese, French, Japanese, and Americans, much better than they understood the difference between Communism and Democracy.

Tuyet was not interested in the political rationale for this tragedy, she wished to destroy these barbarians for taking an innocent man. But all she can do, for a while anyway, is to try to care for her daughters. She thanked the man and silently walked inside with the knowledge of why he died. Nhan can now rest in peace!

I must not dwell in the past or dream of the future, but rather concentrate my mind on the present moment. And that concentration will be focused on my children who have a right to a future. With that in mind, Tuyet decided to send Thu Hoa, the oldest girl, to Saigon for a better education. She can safely stay with our relatives in the city, Tuyet thought. Tailoring and hair styling are in demand and this occupation is very popular with the young girls. That's what we'll do.

The other children were now old enough to help out. My Lien was sixteen, she could help out in the business while the younger girls could care for the one year old baby. With the American Third and Fourth Army Corps occupying Saigon and the Mekong Delta, the restaurant business was flourishing which kept My Lien quite busy especially since Tuyet was still involved with education. French was very popular, thirty percent of the population spoke the language, so things were beginning to look better.

Balzac, the great French author, was considered as one of the greatest novelists of all time with numerous books and essays about France in the nineteenth century. He was called the "French Charles Dickens". His popularity among the Vietnamese was based on their sympathetic feelings toward his positions on French politics. France's lack of bold leadership after Napoleon, had led to ruin and men of quality were being ignored. His writings revealed concern for those who are pushed to one side by society as observed by the youth of France being abandoned by their government with predicted unrest in the future –a very similar situation to the French colonization and Diem government treatment of the native Vietnamese. So the French language and literary works remained popular and Tuyet would be gainfully employed for the foreseeable future.

By the end of 1970 the Communist forces were recovering from the Tet Offensive and the American strikes into Cambodia. During the following February, the North Vietnamese Army inflicted heavy losses on the South Vietnamese Army when they attacked into Laos. The remainder of the year would be spent on a North Vietnam buildup for a new offensive in the 1971-1972 dry season.

The enemy realized that American troop levels had dropped from 540,000 men to 140,000 at the beginning of 1972. In March of that year, the NVA moved south against the South Vietnamese Army that was fighting without American troops on the ground. President Nixon reacted and began to bomb Hanoi and Haiphong again, a move that had been suspended since 1968. By July, American air power and the South Vietnamese Army had stopped the NVA offensive. Peace talks resumed and Kissinger announced that "peace is at hand". Then in December after Nixon's reelection, peace talks stalled because of new demands by South Vietnamese President Nguyen Van Thieu. Le Duc Tho left and went home to Hanoi! The intensive "Christmas Bombings" then continued over Hanoi and Haiphong. Finally in January of 1973, a peace agreement between the United States, North Vietnam, South Vietnam, and the National Liberation Front was signed in Paris as offensive operations by the United

States were stopped. Two months later, in March, all United States troops had left "country". South Vietnam was on its own!

The wartorn country had suffered. In addition to the destruction of industry and communities and the loss of life, 19 million gallons of herbicides and defoliants had been sprayed over 4.2 million acres of South Vietnam. This "Agent Orange" exposed 4.8 million people with 400,000 deaths and disabilities. Five hundred thousand children would be born with birth defects and handicaps. Fortunately for Tuyet and her children, the most affected areas were around the Ho Chi Minh trail that ran along the Truong Son Mountain Range that separates Central Vietnam from Laos and the Cambodian border next to South Vietnam.

In spite of the American departure, My Lien maintained a thriving restaurant business. She had built a loyal following of customers from Phu Loc and neighboring communities, based primarily on the quality food that was offered at reasonable prices. Her mother, Tuyet, was still employed at the local school while the rest of the children attended school and shared responsibilities for the four- year- old Thien Nga.

When it came to personalities, My Lien was strictly business. The tall dark and lean restaurant manager ran a disciplined operation. And at times she could be very difficult in her dealings with suppliers and even customers on occasion, especially men.

But business would continue to grow. The South Vietnamese Army stationed two companies of soldiers in Phu Loc and they frequented the restaurant. Of course the attraction for the visits there was the presence of the very appealing young manager. And the indifferent and cool demeanor of My Lien only made her that much more enchanting. As time went by she became the topic of discussion and one evening while the troops were lounging outside of the restaurant, the captain in charge said that whoever might win her hand will have the wedding paid for by him. See if any of you can get a date.

It might have been an idle boast but one of the soldiers stood up and brazenly put his foot up on the bench and said that he could and would do it! His name was Hieu Tang and he was one of the toughest men in the company. He did not stand out, just average looking but with a rough edge about his personality. Yet he appeared to be a determined and self-disciplined individual.

"I can do it and I will do it. Not only will I get a date but I will get her to like me and then I will marry her!" he shouted.

All of the commotion caught My Lien's attention. She looked out of the window and saw the group facing toward Hieu Tang as he made his remarks. Whoever would marry any of those men, especially the loud one, must be out of their mind or blind, she thought as she just shook her head at the nonsense and went back to work.

The very next day Hieu Tang made an attempt to court My Lien. He sent some small children to deliver flowers in his name. My Lien was offended. She took the flowers and hurled them into the trash can. How dare he act so impudent! I don't know him and I don't want to know him! Several weeks soon passed and he tried once more with candy. My Lien gave the candy to the local children with much fanfare, making sure that he knew it. But he and his mates continued to visit the restaurant and purchase their meals, mainly for him to just be around her. His friends teased him but he didn't care, he was falling in love!

Not much progress was being made and other men started to show interest in the successful young lady. Soon a formal approach was taken by the family that lived next door. They visited Tuyet and requested that she approve the marriage of their son to My Lien. The news spread quickly and one of the nearby children ran to the military base and informed Hieu Tang that someone was asking for My Lien's hand in marriage!

Hieu Tang was not going to let them take away the love of his life. He almost became hysterical with rage as he fastened on his grenade vest and loaded a magazine into his M16A1 rifle. Tuyet was shocked when she opened the door. His incessant pounding had frightened everyone. She tried to calm him down while he loudly demanded that the engagement party come to a stop. The visiting family quietly slipped out the back door terrified that he was going to kill them all or blow up the house. Finally he calmed down after Tuyet softly talked to him and asked his intentions. She promised to discuss his proposal with My Lien but insisted that a formal meeting be held with his family if My Lien was agreeable.

A serious discussion would be in order with My Lien. Realizing that they had a close relationship, Tuyet raised a question that would affect both of their lives permanently. "Would you be willing to obey my wishes if I made the decision regarding your future marriage?" My Lien affectionately replied, "Yes mother, I have always wanted to please you."

The next morning, Tuyet followed her normal routine and left home to teach for the day. But once she was out of sight, she changed direction and headed toward the military encampment. She requested an appointment with Hieu Tang's Commanding Officer. His captain cordially invited her into his office and realized immediately the nature of her visit when she announced her name. "I am here to demand an apology for the threatening and rude behavior of Hieu Tang. He frightened my guests and insulted my family," she angerly said.

"Oh, the men are under a lot of stress, don't take it so seriously," he replied.

"I know that your company is part of the 7th Division of the IV Corps with headquarters in My Tho. I will leave here immediately and go there to lodge a complaint."

This woman is not to be trifled with, I can't afford an investigation, it will imply a lack of discipline here. "Just a minute, I will call Tang here to settle the matter," he pleaded.

When the captain returned, Hieu entered and apologized for his behavior. He was very concerned and puzzled by her quiet manner because he anxiously thought that she would prefer charges. But after the apology and the obvious display of affection for My Lien, Tuyet made a surprising comment.

"If you want to marry my daughter, then ask your parents to come down here to meet me properly as is the custom."

"Oh yes, right away," he excitedly answered. "Sir, I would like to request a short leave of absence to go to Saigon and bring my mother and aunt back to Phu Loc."

"Very well, then the matter is settled?"

"Yes," Tuyet replied, "and rightfully so!"

February was a good month for travel. It was the warm, dry season and peace had come at last throughout the country. So the Hieu Tang family arrived at Phu Loc loaded down with seven trays covered by red silk scarfs. They were a sign of the family's sincerity about the marriage proposal. Tuyet was quite pleased but My Lien was still at the market shopping for food. She had no idea of the visit to her home; her mother had not informed her or even asked her to courteously receive the guests. Tuyet's promise to Hieu had been broken!

My Lan, now eleven years old, ran as hard as she could to the market and told My Lien to come home as quickly as possible. "That guy that you hate is here with his family to ask for your hand in marriage," she breathlessly cried.

"What!!" My Lien loudly answered as the store patrons all stopped and looked. She was furious! "How could mother allow them to come here without talking to me about it?"

The food was left on the counter as she hurriedly left for home. It was a thirty minute walk so she ran as far as she could to stop whatever was being planned. But it was too late, the visitors had left.

"Mother, mother, where are you?" she shouts as she enters the house. Tuyet was just standing there looking at the gifts, how generous she thought. It is a good sign.

"Look at these gifts, My Lien; we are very fortunate."

"Mother, how could you allow that jerk, that madman, to come here with a proposal?" she pleadingly asked.

"My Lien, settle down, look, that man came here with a gun and threatened everybody, nobody will propose to you now. If I don't allow him to marry you, who will? He's liable to kill somebody!"

"I don't care mother, I can't live with him."

Tuyet continued, "Your father is gone, there are only women in the family, we need men in the house again."

My Lien was devastated. She ran out of the house and went to a dry rice field and sat down. For hours she wept until finally the sun went down and My Lan called her for dinner. She slowly got up, wiped her face, and headed home. It would take some time, but she would make the sacrifice and please her mother – an unselfish and noble act of perfect charity!

During the United States withdrawal, President Thieu of South

Vietnam had been allowed to stay in power. The treaty had also allowed the 145,000 man North Vietnamese army to stay in South Vietnam while the United States had sixty days to leave with billions of dollars of military equipment left behind. An election to reunite the country was to be managed by a "National Council of Reconciliation".

The peace agreement did not have a chance! Viet Cong took over three hundred villages on the day before the signing of the treaty. Then on the first day of the agreement South Vietnam started to drive the Viet Cong out. All during 1974, Communists were arrested and put in jail by Thieu's government and the elections were not held. But the failure to win the hearts and minds of the rural areas in South Vietnam was a major reason why the South Vietnamese army would eventually fail to win the war. So the men in the South Vietnam army were based as close as possible to home to instill in them the desire to be determined to protect their homeland. Hieu Tang was one of these men.

It was just about the end of the dry season when they got married. The weather was perfect this 28th day of April, 1974. My Lien wore an all white silk Ao Dai with a red flower in her hair and a brilliant bejeweled crown. She looked beautiful! Hieu was dressed in his best uniform and beamed with pride. Everyone was happy for the newlyweds. The house was filled with joy and laughter. Several days later, Thu Hoa would bring home her boyfriend, a young military pilot, Nuyen Trac.

There was a large South Vietnam air base close by at Soc Trang that housed the 225th and 227th Helicopter Squadrons with Huey aircraft and the 249th Squadron with CH-47 Chinook aircraft. Between that and the mechanized rifle companies of the 7th Division that had M113 Armored Personnel carriers deployed, the countryside around Phu Loc must have been quite active with flyovers and patrols.

The next year on January 8, 1975, the status quo came to an end. North Vietnam began a major offensive and the Saigon army began to fall back. The general that had been defending Pleiku fled by plane leaving the 200,000 man army leaderless. They became a terrorized mob and fled toward Danang on the coast. Upon reaching the beaches, men threw away their weapons and uniforms and tried to swim to the American ships.

The scene repeated itself elsewhere and the society began to disintegrate from the internal corruption of the government and army – soldiers had not been paid, military equipment had been sold to the Viet Cong and the black market, while government officials made millions of United States dollars. On April 30, Saigon fell and the war ended. Immediately, a North Vietnam Military Management Committee was set up to run the South Vietnamese government. The National Liberation Front including Viet Cong and civilians with their Provisional Revolutionary Government were swiftly removed from power to allow for the rapid unification of the country under Communist rule.

On May 5, 1975, My Lien had her first baby, a boy they would call Thao. Her oldest sister, Thu Hoa, was also pregnant with her first baby, a boy. She had come back to Phu Loc after a narrow escape from Saigon when the North Vietnamese army had begun the attack on the city. I must tell her story!

Back on January 8, the NVA invaded the south with twenty divisions to begin a two- year offensive, but Saigon would fall in fifty-five days. The United States did not initiate "severe retaliation action" as promised when the Paris Peace treaty was violated.

From the start of the campaign to April 20, the cities and regions fell like dominos; Ba Me Thuot, Quang Tri Province, Tam Ky, city of Hue, Danang, Xuan Loc, with other cities being abandoned by the South Vietnamese forces. Starting on the 14th of April, 14,000 homeless children were airlifted by the United States to America.

An uneasy quiet settled around Saigon from April 20 to April 26, the enemy was making plans for the final push. A three pronged attack by sixteen NVA divisions would begin on the 28th. That evening, the bombing of Tan Son Nhat air base on the western side of the city began with A37Dragonfly light attack aircraft. Thu Hoa and her husband could hear the explosions from their safe haven hideout. The next day the bombardment continued with rocket and artillery concentration on the Defense Attack Office command control center in Saigon. Sappers and infantry had infiltrated Go Gap and Cu Chi a few miles northwest of Saigon.

Thu Hoa and Nuyen were frightened as the enemy forces circled around the city. They could now hear the explosions from the artillery and rocket fire. "We must get out of here," she urged.

"How are you going to do it, you're eight months pregnant?" Nuyen pleaded.

"If we're captured, you may be executed or imprisoned for being a South Vietnamese pilot."

"All right, we'll leave at dark and try to get around the fence."

They waited anxiously all day while the explosions came closer and closer. Soon the streets overhead were sending waves of concussions down through the shelter with debris falling off of the ceiling and walls. They could hear people screaming up above and running randomly from place to place. "Stay close to me, I'll put this blanket over our heads," he shouted as he wrapped the blanket around her and held her tight.

The passing of the day seemed like eternity with the never ending continuous explosions being heard far off then coming directly overhead with ear-shattering noise. When night approached, Nuyen helped Thu Hoa to stand up. Her legs were cramped from sitting all day in a small corner of the room. They made it to the street entrance and cautiously went outside. Thu Hoa was shocked at the destroyed buildings and damaged streets. Bodies were strewn everywhere as they carefully made their way past the craters and fallen bricks. "I can't climb over that barbed wire fence," she cried.

"Wait a minute. I see a small gap between the pole and the fence. See if you can crawl through the opening."

She laid down and slid on her back as he pulled up the fence. She was through. Quickly they made their way to a distant underground shelter that had been made by Hieu Tang. They were safe! Nuyen would take leave of his wife after the baby was born. He traveled back to Saigon disguised as a peasant and took refuge with his family. Tuyet reluctantly agreed to have Thu Hoa move to Saigon to join her husband.

The war was over at last. We all saw the famous pictures of the last helicopter on the top of the building as refugees climbed single file up the ladder to escape. Grandmother must have worried about the future of the family because she would often say, "They left us behind!"

So many lives were lost. An American song that had originated in the

United States antiwar movement and then had become a favorite among the soldiers now seemed to express the sentiment of both the Vietnamese people and the Americans. It was called, "Where Have All The Flowers Gone?", and it concluded that the result of war was the loss of all the young soldiers to the grave, yet the world never learned.

In July 1976, the newly elected National Assembly meets for the formal unification of North and South Vietnam. The impact on the south is northern dominance of the business of government. As the totalitarian government combines with the lowered standard of living, the people take interest in a new approach to a life of quality – emigration!

Well look who's here! I arrive on the scene on May 6, 1977, the second child of My Lien and Hieu Tang. They will name me Cungdiem after a movie actress that they had enjoyed watching at the theatre. I was now officially a citizen of the Socialist Republic of Vietnam!

CHAPTER 3

CAN THO

"All Is Lost"

Hieu was a good husband and father but he wanted to do more. He had never accepted the defeat of South Vietnam and he wanted to continue the struggle. The Communists must be driven out of the country and other people felt the same way. As time passed and opinions were shared, a covert group soon emerged. His friends and colleagues would begin to meet secretly to discuss politics and even violent measures to meet their goals of self government. They would have to be discreet when communicating outside of the meetings; infiltrators and informers were everywhere. The first meeting had a good turnout and ideas were shared and debated over the type of mission that they would pursue and the details needed to achieve that commitment.

Hieu knew most of the members at the first meeting and he recognized the names of the other participants. He felt safe about the loyalty of these people but he wasn't sure about everyone. The group arranged a date and time for the next meeting but with the condition that the meetings would be held at different locations each time to avoid being noticed.

The second meeting occurred soon after but one person was missing, it was a trap! Government troops had surrounded the small hut after the traitor informed them of the location and time. They broke through the door and held their weapons on the men. Hieu and the others were arrested with their hands tied behind their backs and carried off to a holding pen for interrogation. When Hieu did not return home, his family was worried. As the days passed with no information other than a bystander's witness of the arrest, My Lien was panic stricken!

For two months the family was devastated, not knowing whether Hieu was in prison or executed. But they finally received news that he was being transferred with the others to a new location. My Lien went from one official to another to request information but she received nothing, either they did not know or they refused to share anything about him.

Then one dark and stormy night with lightning and thunder crashing around the house, Tuyet looked out of one of the windows and saw moving shadows. She raised the oil lantern to get a better view but saw nothing. A short time later, they all heard some commotion and gun shots. She hurriedly gathered her daughters and children and sent them to the back of the house. "Get whatever you can find to defend yourselves," she whispered. All became quiet than a loud knock on the door frightened everyone. "Don't answer it mother," one of them said. It was a crowd of men outside and the leader began to shout, "Let us in or we'll blow up your house!" Tuyet decided that the women and children had a better chance of survival if they let the men enter the house. We'll all be dead if they blow us up, she thought. Maybe they won't harm us, we'll see what they want.

Tuyet opened the door, the leader pushed inside followed by two more men. They were all dressed the same with gray and white clothing and conical straw hats. Two additional men stayed outside and guarded the entrance. The leader looked around the house and asked if any men lived there. Tuyet hesitated and then said "No".

"Good, this will make it easy for you women," he snarled. "Give me all the deeds to your properties, everything you own." With that remark he held his pistol to Tuyet's head. Seeing the danger, the daughters gathered every document they could find and gave them to him. We can always start over My Lien thought but not if we're killed. The men then left immediately without saying a word, like black panthers on the prowl for victims!

One of the propaganda tools that the Communists used to promote victory was the promise of land and housing. If the people would help to get the Americans out of Vietnam, land and housing would be redistributed from the people of means to the poor peasants - a perfect example of Marxist philosophy and socialization to the extreme!

Decades of work disappeared overnight! Our home and business properties were gone that had been developed beginning with my great grandparents from China. All the love and sacrifices to build the restaurant, billiard bar, and our home were taken from us by ruthless government people. I was an infant but I can imagine how lost everyone felt. Where were we going to live? And where was my father?

It didn't take long. A few days later a group of vicious people came to claim the property. The only recourse grandmother Tuyet had was to take her daughters and grandchildren to a little shack in the rice field that had been built for the farmers to use during harvest time. The roof was made of woven palm leaves and the walls were a combination of clay mixed with binding rice husks (the hard shell that contains the rice).

The rainy season was on us and the roof leaked. My family was so crowded in this small place that they had to sleep while sitting up and leaning against the walls. Everyone just tried to pass the cold wet days with patience while being confined to this terrible condition. Grandmother Tuyet could not sleep well, she was constantly thinking of ways to improve the situation. Her daughters deserved better and she was going to do something about it!

At the first break in the weather, Tuyet and one of her daughters worked up on the roof to repair the holes and leaks. They then added rooms to the shack by blending clay subsoil and rice husks with water while having a neighbor's buffalo trample it until the combination was well mixed. It was a slow process as layers would be set up for the walls and then be allowed to dry before the next course was added. This ancient form of "cobbing" would make thick walls that would hold heat in cold weather and cool air in the summer. Bamboo stalks were then collected and cut and lashed together to make the beds. Some bowls and glasses were made by cutting above and below the nodes of the stalk. Even a flute was made to try and make music.

The next thing to be concerned about was money. Tuyet applied at the school to be reinstated and she was accepted. The daughters all baked cakes to sell at the market in the late afternoons returning in time to prepare supper for their mother and the family. Four months went by this way and Tuyet had now earned enough money to send Thu Huong and My Lan to Saigon to attend beauty school. My Lien was still searching for Hieu Tang, he had been gone the entire time and she still knew nothing about his location. Nga and Sau were still teenagers, so they attended the local school in town. Thao and I remained as toddlers with My Lien at the shack.

Some semblance of routine began to form, My Lien was at the market one cloudy day, nothing out of the ordinary. Suddenly, she overheard a conversation that seemed to be gossip but it was a rumor about the prisoners. She became so upset and nervous that she dropped her bag of groceries before paying the cashier. I must check this out, she thought. Knowing where Hieu was before he departed, she ran to the local precinct and went inside. The tall, dark tattooed officer pulled down his straw hat and glared at My Lien with a look of hatred. "What do you want woman?" he asked in a deep voice. My Lien was frightened but she pulled herself together and politely said, "Excuse me, sir, I just heard about the prisoners that you captured a few months ago. Can you tell me where they are now? One of them is my husband."

The sullen guard slammed his fist down on the bamboo desk, nearly breaking it in half. "They're all dead by now, and even if they are alive, they are all near death with broken arms and legs from the interrogations," he shouted.

"Please sir, take this grocery money for your coffee and tea, I just want to know where they are," she pleaded. "I have two young children and they miss their father."

"Is that all you got? It's not enough for a cigarette. My partner needs some too!" Then he laughs and says, "Go away, when you have more, come back and I'll tell you more."

My Lien felt helpless. She slowly walked out and headed for school where her mother was teaching class. She waited until break time then approached Tuyet but she couldn't restrain herself.

"What's the matter daughter? Why are you crying?" Tuyet asked and quickly continued, "Are the men safe?"

"Yes," My Lien replied as she sobbed, "yes, they are safe but they know where my husband is and they won't tell me unless I give them money."

"All right, now calm down, have a seat while I go and talk to some of the teachers. They'll lend me the money that you'll need."

My Lien suddenly felt relieved but continued to cry out of gratitude. She had mixed emotions; she didn't know how she felt. With her heart beating fast from the excitement, she felt happy for the support of the teachers, yet sad for her husband's situation and worried about his whereabouts. As she thought about her dilemma, Tuyet came running with a handful of money. "Here, take this money, it's 600 dong so it's worth a lot. Now hurry to those people and tell me what happened when I get home." My Lien smiled through her tears and left with joy. She was filled with hope!

When she arrived at the office, the tattooed man wasn't there. This time it was a short man with a deceitful smile on his face. My Lien didn't like his looks and hesitated. "Hey woman, you got the money? I'll let you know where your husband is if you do." Then he laughed, a lewd brazen laugh and said, "I need you to smile for me, I hate to see a pretty face looking at me so sad." He laughed again.

My Lien stiffened up. She was afraid of this evil man but her thoughts were different. She wanted to rip him apart and feed him to the tigers. I've got to compose myself. She cleared her throat and pleasantly responded, "Please sir, I need to know where my husband is, my children need their father." And then she cried.

The guard was unimpressed. "Your husband might not have any hands or legs anymore. Why don't I be your children's father instead?" Once more he laughed. He was enjoying himself and exerting his power over her. Now she begged him. The pleading continued for another ten minutes until the tattooed guard walked into the office. Seeing the money, and being of higher rank, he ordered the officer to stand down. "Let her know where he is – you jerk!"

"All right woman, the prison is located four hours away from here by foot. It's in the jungle, you have to cross the two lakes, go through the bamboo forest and then you'll see the prison. Just tell them we sent you, then you can see your husband."

My Lien gets up to leave, she is wet from the nervous perspiration. As she turns toward the door, she notices them counting the money and both of them were laughing.

She completely forgot about the groceries, that was unimportant. The news of her husband after all these months made her excited and anxious about a visit to see him. Realizing that it was now six o'clock in the evening, she ran home and found the family already seated for dinner. As usual, a healthy meal of rice with two dishes of steamed vegetables and a bowl of watermelon was being served by Tuyet when My Lien opened the door. Thien Nga, the youngest sister now eight years old, was always outspoken with the family. Perhaps it was because she was the youngest and somewhat spoiled. She lived up to her reputation when she blurted out to My Lien, "What happened to the food today? We don't have any meat, did you lose the money?"

Tuyet interjected before My Lien could answer and said while serving the food, "My Lien found her husband, tomorrow she and I are going to look for him, isn't that wonderful?" Then she lowered her voice to a more serious tone and said, "I want everyone to stay home and watch the children when we leave the first thing in the morning. It will probably take us all day, but we'll be back home as soon as possible."

The early morning frost on the ground gave Tuyet a chill as she got up to dress. There had been no effort to bank up the fire for the night and the four o'clock hour was still dark. It should warm up after sunrise, she supposed. "My Lien," she whispered, "wake up." My Lien made out her mother's figure in the gloom and slowly moved her son's arm away from her shoulder. Being careful to avoid waking him and Cungdiem, she slipped out of the room and packed some food and water and counted what little money she had to bring along for the trip.

For me of course, being an infant, I would not have remembered any of this story, but I remember the events well from being told many times about their trials and sacrifices. How blessed was my father to have such a courageous wife as My Lien and also my brave grandmother. They were so loyal to him, they never gave up.

Let me recount this adventure as best as I can. The two women silently left their home and quietly slipped through the town before the market opened and people started their day. They didn't need to be asked a lot of questions; the gossip could spread and get into the wrong hands. It would be a long journey, so they tried to pace themselves as they began to pass the rice fields.

The fields seemed endless, square patches of green rice shoots, separated by irrigation ditches like a quilt patchwork. They looked like huge fields of grass. Sometimes our travelers would pass thin strands of trees that divided the rice fields, a mix of short palm and hardwoods. Occasionally they would cross the ditches on flat wooden bridges made of small sticks laid across two large poles. To get over the larger canals, they had to carefully walk across the "cau khi" bridge or "monkey bridge." It was constructed of bamboo poles and they had to cross by walking across a single bamboo pole supported by bamboo frames while holding onto a horizontal bamboo pole that was mounted slightly higher.

After hiking along for about two hours, they started to hear soft musical sounds. As they got closer, they noticed a water buffalo standing still with its huge curved horns watching them approach. But on top of the back of the docile beast was a small boy pleasantly playing a flute. "Isn't that nice," My Lien said, "not a worry in the world. Look at the birds too mother, flying free in the sky. Wouldn't it be nice if we could be free like that?"

"Yes," Tuyet replied, "maybe someday we will be free."

Finally they pass a lake. It was noon and the journey was taking longer then they had been told it would be by the guards. After they crossed another wooden stick bridge, the soil became muddy and wet. Leeches were everywhere, clinging to their clothes. My Lien kept feeling her pants, she was afraid of the bloodsucking creatures. By three o'clock in the afternoon, they had passed the second lake and decided to rest.

They sat under a star fruit tree and ate some of its fruit, only the ripe yellow ones. The star shaped food was sweet and juicy; they ate the whole thing including the slightly waxy skin. It tasted like a combination of orange, grapefruit, and papaya – very healthy. "Mother, we must not stay here too long, I want to see my husband."

"Yes My Lien, I understand, but be patient, I'm a little older than you."

Once again they trod along and approach the bamboo forest. The trees are tall with straight narrow banana or green colored trunks. At the top, the thin long leaves fan out from the limbs. They create a canopy over the floor of the forest. It was very quiet and peaceful with leaves now and then dropping softly from the trees like snow flakes. Two more miles are covered and then they see a clearing.

There was the prison! Nothing more than a shack divided into small rooms with no doors. They stood there and observed the barb wire fence and broken glass bottles that surrounded the place. Off to the side of the compound was a tall observation tower. Guards with rifles in their hands watched the two women with field glasses. My Lien glanced up and shuddered.

Tuyet took a quick survey of the place. Some prisoners were seen working a garden. Their clothing was torn from wear and rot and their hair was long and unkempt. Many other men were lying inside the door openings, some crying in pain and others staring blankly into space. The few men that could stand were only able to limp around. My Lien became distraught and slowly started to weep, she couldn't control her emotion while thinking of Hieu being there. Tuyet nudged My Lien with her elbow and abruptly said, "Stop, we're here! We can't show any weakness. These people are ruthless, they have no mercy – be brave! That's the only thing they'll respect."

Upon reaching the gate, the women were challenged by the armed guard. "Go home you two – there's no place for you here!" Tuyet spoke up to the tall dark sentry and said, "Sir, I would like to speak to whoever is in charge here."

"What do you want," he sternly asked. Tuyet knew that she would have to bribe him to even get through the gate. "Please take this money, it's all I have," hoping that he would not search her. She continued, "We were sent here by another of your fellow officers. He said that my son was a prisoner here," hoping that the illusion of being his mother would gain

BAMBOO FOREST

Courtesy of Public Domain Pictures by Peter Griffin

MONKEY BRIDGE

Courtesy of Wikimedia Commons by Kelcey Kinjo

some sympathy. The guard counted the money and replied, "Maybe next time you can bring some more. What's his name?"

"It is Hieu Tang," she anxiously answered.

"Oh, that young one, he's troublesome. We just questioned him, he might not be strong enough to visit with you. Come back tomorrow." He laughed and looked over at the other guards who then joined in with the fun.

"Please sir, we live very far from here, it took all day to get here from our home," and then she cried. The strain was finally reaching Tuyet.

"Ok, I can't stand to see frail women cry, follow me."

Through the gate they went with tower guns trained on them while other guards behind barricades joined in with their threatening weapons. My Lien froze in place and then cautiously moved ahead.

The glare from the sunset illuminated the surroundings with an eerie orange color and then bright red as the sun began to sink behind the trees. Two of the Communist soldiers came through one of the doors awkwardly carrying a man. His face was covered with blood and bruises were around the eyes. They dropped him in front of the door and left.

"It's him! It's him, mother!" My Lien was in shock, she couldn't move her legs to reach him. She tried to wipe her tears with shaking hands and then felt faint. Tuyet quickly moved over and caught her as she started to fall. Tuyet calls out, "Hieu, how do you feel, do you know who we are?" The gate guard was standing close by and he shouted, "Wake up traitor, your family is here and they can only stay for thirty minutes."

Hieu slowly forced himself to sit up with the help of Tuyet and My Lien. He wiped the blood away from his eyes so that he could see these angels of mercy. Their voices had given them away and he spoke to them through his tears. "I thought that I was going to die here and never see my family again. I am so happy to see you." My Lien embraced her husband and then poured out a drink of water. Tuyet wiped the blood and tears away from his face with her hankerchief.

After he settled down and composed himself, they prepared some of the food for him that they brought along from home. "You must be starving," Tuyet said as she noticed the emaciated state that he was in, "do they feed you at all?"

"No," he whispered, "some men are dying of hunger and from the beatings they get all the time. They will die if their families don't take care of them. I've been living on what I could get from the garden, and I share the rice that the guards throw in the garbage. There's a pig trough that they sometimes throw the leftovers into, we try to get there before the pigs do. But I get desperate sometimes and eat worms and lice off my clothes."

Hearing that, Tuyet took the rest of the food and gave it to the other prisoners. They gathered around and ate the small meals like starving wolves, devouring every morsel as fast as they could. Tuyet waited a respectful amount of time and then asked Hieu, "How long are they going to keep you here, are they going to release you at all?"

"We don't know," he feebly replied, "it's about forty of us here and they keep taking us outside, one by one, to question every day, and then they beat us until we talk or they keep repeating the beatings until we die."

That did it for Tuyet. She had to walk away from the men as she began to shed tears. I must find the soldier who brought us through the gate. While heading toward the front office she observed that all of the men were confined to a total space of 20 by forty feet or about four by five feet per man. And she heard that they could only go outside twice a day to relieve themselves unless allowed to work the garden, if able. She couldn't wait to reach the front office; the stench of body odors, human waste, and death, made the heavy air unbearable. At last she found him, "Sir, when can I come back to see my son again?"

"You can come to visit once a month but make sure you bring more money, we need some for tea." He laughed once again with that sadistic and scheming sneer and said, "You know what will happen to your son if you don't." Tuyet couldn't wait to leave, "Thank you sir, you have been very helpful."

On the way back to My Lien and the group, she observed that the sky was getting dark. "We better leave now My Lien, we have to go through the bamboo forest and cross the two lakes again. It will not be easy finding our way and we will have to be on the lookout for any wild animals hunting in the area now. There will be king cobras and giant pythons along with those fresh water crocodiles by the lakes. The clouded leopard shouldn't bother us, they're small cats about two to three feet long. The big tigers don't go any farther south than the Central Highlands, mostly the Truong Son range. But there have been cases of maneaters."

"Stop mother, my nerves are shattered now, we'll be fine."

My Lien placed a small amount of money in Hieu's pocket and set the rest of the food beside him knowing that the grateful group of prisoners would protect him from predators. The tears were still flowing as she said goodby and he responded, "I love you so much, take care of the children and tell them that I love them very much." It took most of the night to make the journey home. They passed through the bamboo forest and around the lakes while listening to the animal cries of the hunters and the hunted. Every shadow was watched closely and carefully avoided. At last they were home, the children had been awakened and were being read to by their aunts while they waited for their mother. It was a happy reunion. Tuyet and My Lien were safely home.

For the entire next month, My Lien worked hard to save part of her earnings. In her spare time she prepared a lot of dried fruit, shrimp, and beef jerky. Clothing was carefully selected from his wardrobe and she decided to bring something along to help him pass the time. He was quite good at art and he knew how to embroider, so she included some white fabric, thread, and needle.

This time she would go alone. Tuyet had to return to her classes and take care of the grandchildren. She left extra early, just as the predawn light emerged. The tiresome journey was wrought with more bad news – the prisoners were to be relocated to another camp site, an additional four hours for her to travel. But she would be bound and determined to visit him once a month if she had to go as far away as Hanoi.

Hieu met her again with tears, she gave him hope. When asked by My Lien about the relocation, he said, "Every time they move us, we will walk tall, to show our defiance."

"You and your friends are so brave! I will bring extra food for them each time because I know you value their friendship. You need to stick together to survive."

"Yes, they beat us and torture us. Sometimes they will wrap a man in barb wire for hours. Or place a knee in the back with the man face down to dislocate the shoulders. I could go on – the worst one is when they tie the prisoner's hands and a Bowie knife behind his back with the Bowie knife pointed inward toward his back. Then they would haul the prisoner up against a tree and start pushing against his chest."

"Please Hieu, tell me no more."

"Yes, maybe it won't be so bad at the next place, I have hope."

The year passed by quickly. My Lien would be faithful in her visits. She met some of the wives of the prisoners and managed to travel with them back and forth. Now they would gather at the prison entrance together and talk through the fence to their waiting spouses until the gates were opened. Back home, Tuyet's income wasn't quite enough. The daughters all held odd jobs to help My Lien meet the demands of her husband's captors.

The next year, 1978, was a banner year for the exodus from Vietnam. Massive numbers of people were streaming out of the country. And for just cause, in addition to the new government, a Third Indochina War had started on the border with China. This so-called Sino-Vietnamese War lasted for a brief period in 1979 with thousands of casualties on both sides. After the Soviet Union had signed a mutual defense treaty with Vietnam, China became defiant toward the USSR. Vietnam had invaded and occupied Cambodia to end the Khmer Rouge regime. They also conducted raids along the northern border into Chinese territory. China reacted and invaded Vietnam along the northern border but did not sustain the effort in spite of the 300,000 man army. As they retreated toward their homeland, a "scorched earth policy" was conducted with the burning of villages, destruction of roads, and the general upheaval of the infrastructure. Refugees poured south into Southeast Asian camps looking for new homes.

In the summer of 1979, Tuyet visited Ho Chi Minh city during school break to visit her oldest daughter Thu Hoa. She and her three sons were now living with her mother-in-law because Nuyen Trac, her husband, had fled by plane to the United States. Tuyet immediately noticed that Thu Hoa was being treated like a maid. She had to cook, clean, and take care of the house. And to add insult to injury, the mother-in-law was still not satisfied with her work. As Tuyet approached the front door, she noticed her grandchildren playing outside with the neighborhood children. Then when she entered, Thu Hoa was on her knees scrubbing the floor while the mother-in-law sat on the sofa along with the sister-in-law who was polishing her nails. When Tuyet greeted them, they ignored her and walked away.

In spite of the reception, Tuyet was happy to see her daughter but she struggled to hide her tears when she realized the hardship that Thu Hoa was enduring. So, being true to form, Tuyet began to help her daughter and then they prepared dinner. The seating arrangement was insolent – the in-laws sat at the dining room table with the grandchildren while Tuyet and Thu Hoa had to sit at a little table in the kitchen. After the stressful visit, Tuyet reflected on Thu Hoa's situation. Why should she be treated like a slave for that rich, self-centered family? She's a daughter of a well known professor and should be treated with the dignity that she deserves. Tuyet was broken-hearted once more. I've got to develop a plan for her – I'm going to get her out of Vietnam!

It wasn't too long after that visit that Sau, her fourth daughter, became ill. She had developed a high fever and now began to have seizures. Finally, one night around nine o'clock, the beautiful seventeen year old passed away. This was too much! Too many bad things are happening in too short a period of time. Is it the bad magic they call black voodoo, Tuyet pondered? I've heard that they kidnap pregnant women, kill the mother and take the unborn baby to soak in alcohol. Then they drink the potion to gain the power of black magic so that they can place a curse on someone. But what bothers me is their practice of kidnapping an innocent teenaged girl. Then they cut off her head before the soul leaves the body so that her eyes will give them the eyes to another world and predictions of the future.

Tuyet did not appear to be rational. Perhaps the long period of stress had taken its toll. Would they dig her daughter out of the grave and cut off her head? I must make a plan, Tuyet thought. In our culture we believe that seven times seven equals forty-nine so that after forty-nine days the soul will leave the body to depart to another world. Then the voodoo practice will not work!

So Tuyet decided to stand watch. She had relatives guard the grave during the day while she and one of her daughters would stand by during the night. She wasn't concerned about the graveyard shift but after a week strange things began to happen. Noises occurred at night and the odor from a burning yucca plant seemed to permeate the grave yard. Tuyet wondered where the source of the scent was located, they were ten miles from the main road, no houses were in the area, and there was nothing but rice fields. In spite of the noises, odors, and the howling of wolves, Tuyet stood her vigil and she stood it for 49 days. On the next day, they prepared a small food and fruit offering for her daughter, said goodbye, and left. She was too young but Tuyet believed that she had to be in a better place.

It was really raining hard outside! And did the children love it! They were running and singing in the rain, bare naked. It was an example of the purity of innocents. They had no worries, or concerns. Tuyet stood nearby under shelter and watched the joy of youth as she decided to develop the plan for Thu Hoa and the three children to get out of Vietnam. She would travel to Ho Chi Minh City and pretend to take the children and Thu Hoa back to Phu Loc for summer vacation. From there they would leave immediately for America – but how, where, and who could she trust?

CHAPTER 4

SAIGON

"Let Us Leave"

It seemed like a perfect plan, it had to be! Taking the grandchildren and Thu Hoa for vacation would open the door to freedom. Tuyet did not hesitate, she walked down to the market the very next day. The rains had stopped and she carefully picked her way around the puddles of water until she reached the relative that she knew could help her. They had a mutual friend in Saigon, as she preferred to call the city, and his name was Ong Sau. We'll have to keep this plan secret, if too many people become informed, it will leak out and everyone will get arrested. The sentence is one year in jail for attempting to escape to another country. Tuyet then decided to visit Ong Sau and pick up Thu Hoa and the children for their summer visit to Phu Loc.

That evening after dinner, she discussed the idea with her daughters. They retired to the bedroom away from the children and Tuyet began. "Tomorrow I will go to Saigon and visit a man called Ong Sau. He will help your sister and her children escape to America. She must be taken out of slavery and given a new life." They were all shocked at this bold and dangerous statement. The whole family could go to prison and who knows what the Communists would do to them in captivity. "How much will it cost?" one of them said, "Nobody does anything for free."

Tuyet remained quiet until she had their attention. "When your father was alive he gave me some bags of gold and said not to use them unless it was an emergency or a matter of life and death. So I didn't, instead he buried them for me to keep them safe. If the gold doesn't cover expenses, I'll borrow money from relatives and tell them that I'm starting a new business.

The sudden turn of events unsettled everyone. No one was able to sleep well that night, they realized the terrible risk of the unknown obstacles during the journey. On the other hand, if they didn't take their chances, life here wasn't worth living – especially when they would have to witness the miserable life of their children in a communist society. The emotional pain of this existence would be worse than the pain from swallowing broken glass.

She knew exactly where to dig, so Tuyet waited until just before dawn and then went out to a large star fruit tree. After digging about two feet down, she hit metal. It was the box and it had her husband's initials on it. There was a letter inside that surprised her. It was a note from her husband.

"Dear Tuyet,

If you get this letter and I am no longer by your side, please forgive me. I didn't have much to offer you when we were first married and now I have left you alone on this earth to fight the injustices of society by yourself. But don't worry, I will still watch over you and the children, you are my heart beat. When we were in school, I often thought about just taking you in my dreams and escaping to a carefree world.

I love to watch you smile, it fills my heart with joy. I love to smell your long black beautiful hair with the sweet fragrance of vanilla. Please forgive me if I had to leave you first and use the gold wisely because that is all I can give you now.

Goodbye my love, and tell our children that I will always watch over them until we meet again.

Your husband

Huynh van Nhan"

She sobbed bitterly. He was needed now more than ever. The hole was then refilled and smoothed over to conceal the site. She took a deep breath, wiped her eyes and made a vow to her husband in a voice that carried across the rice fields, "My love, I will use the gold wisely, our daughter needs the money so much to escape from here. She has no future as a slave for that Witch Of A Mother In-Law who's stealing her youth!!!"

It was always great weather during the late summer days and this day was no exception. As the morning sun climbed above the hillside Tuyet packed food for her grandchildren. "Wake up My Lien, I want you to watch the house along with your usual routine. Now be sure and take care of everything, I'll be back in three days." She then walked out of the house into the dry morning air and to create the impression she needed, she said out loud, "I'm leaving now for my vacation in Saigon. You children be good and take care of yourselves. When I get back, I want to hear that you've been on your best behavior."

The bus station was only thirty minutes away. She climbed on board and walked to the last seat in the rear of the bus. Her backpack had money and some gold in it and she wanted to guard it by not having people behind her. Professional pickpockets were everywhere and she knew their tricks. They could bump into you and cut your pocket or bag with a razor blade before you knew it. Then a second person would knock you down as if by accident. All would be over in less than a minute.

Saigon's city lights were just ahead. It was eight o'clock and Tuyet was nervous and hungry. But she needed to find Ong Sau as soon as possible, it was too risky walking around in the city with the money and gold. Not only could she be robbed, the Communists might pick her up and definitely take her possessions. She looked up the address and asked some people at a coffee bar for directions. One person was kind enough to show her the way.

She was quite taken back when she arrived. The house was an old shack with a straw roof and palm leaf walls. It looked abandoned; half of the fence had fallen down, the flowers were all dried up and wilted, grass was high, and the place looked dark inside. Tuyet was afraid it was a trick, a deception to get her alone. She felt like someone was watching her.

She ran down the street to a motel where there were a lot of people milling around. I better rent a room for the night she thought. Some food and a shower should help me sleep. But what am I going to do with this large backpack when I go out to eat supper? Tuyet walked back to the service desk and asked for a sewing needle and some thread. Back at the room she locked the door, pulled down the mosquito net, and proceeded to cut out one of her pockets. She then sewed it on the inside of her pants to frustrate any pickpocket attempts. Her leg would be sensitive to any movement or touch by an intruder. Now she felt comfortable about her money. She placed the cash and gold into the hidden pocket and left for an outdoor restaurant that had carry-out food. A Pho bowl of beef was ordered. I better not order anything else, the extra money might be needed tomorrow. As expected, when she returned to the room, the backpack had been searched thoroughly by someone at the motel. You can't trust anyone these days, everybody needs money after the war and they'll do anything to get it. At least I'm forewarned.

A fitful sleep that made the night seem long was caused by the city street noises that were not familiar to Tuyet. They awakened her from time to time. When she checked out the next morning, she showed the address of Ong Sau to the desk clerk. "Oh yes, they have relocated the street to a different part of town, that area is deserted now. Your address is no longer valid."

I'm not going to waste my money on a cycle rickshaw or motorbike taxi, she mused, I'll walk until I find someone to direct me. She passed a street food vendor and ordered a Banh Mi made of meat and vegetables wrapped in bread. "Would you add a little extra soy sauce and hot pepper," she asked the woman food handler, "I like it a little more spicy." She ate as she walked and was overwhelmed by the Saigon traffic. Cars, motorcycles, bicycles, rickshaws, and all sorts of vehicles were crowding the streets with dust and engine exhaust lying thick and heavy. It was an irritant to Tuyet's respiratory system that was accustomed to fresh air. After a while she began to cough and then her nose started to bleed. I better sit down and rest in this park that I'm near.

It was beautiful! An oasis in the middle of all this pollution - a few small ponds with a waterfall, and flowers everywhere, marigolds to rose gardens. It was the Thao Cam Vien Park, home of the zoo and botanical gardens on Nguyen Binh Khiem street in northeast Ho Chi Minh city.

Tuyet asked a man for directions as he walked by. She was fortunate,

REUNIFICATION HALL

NOTRE DAME CATHEDRAL

Courtesy of Wikimedia Commons by author Amore Mio

he knew the location of the relatively new street. Ong Sau's house was only a mile away in the better part of town. She would have to hurry, it was already noon and the children would have to be picked up by two o'clock to meet the three pm bus departure. A fast walk and a quick run across the intersections would be needed. It was a shame that she didn't have more time to enjoy the sights. She hurried down XO Viet Nghe Tinh boulevard, made a left turn on Hai Ba Trung, then a right on to Nguyen Du and passed the Notre Dame Cathedral with its twin spires, the largest church ever built in the French empire. Continuing south, she passed Reunification Hall, the former Presidential Palace of President Diem which had the distinction of having the palace gates knocked down by a North Vietnamese tank during the siege of Saigon.

At last she was there. It was an imposing brick home about five to eight years old with a gated entrance to the driveway. She noticed a man watering the plants and asked if Ong Sau lived there. "Who are you?" he queried, wondering how she knew his familiar nickname that was only used by his business partners. And then loudly, "What do you want?"

"My name is Tuyet. My relatives sent me here to see you, I am from Phu Loc."

Upon hearing that he immediately extended a courtesy as he put the hose down and walked toward the gate. "Come in, come in, you've traveled a long distance, come in and relax with some tea." Tuyet noticed that he looked all around as they entered the front porch, to be sure that no one had followed her or that covert Communist officials had not been standing watch over his home.

Once inside, he locked the door and brought out his tea set. The fancy white clay teapot with blue motifs called hoa lam was sitting in a carved out coconut shell. That would hold the heat in the tea for hours. Tuyet noticed that this beautiful glazed white teapot with hand-painted blue butterfly flowers had an elegant handle and pouring spout. It must have come from Bat Trang where they make beautiful ceramics and have a ceramic and pottery village. But she wondered how he ever got up there to get this tea set. The town is thirteen kilometers southeast of Hanoi! While she was musing over his apparent savoir faire and affluence, he mentioned that he could taste any tea and identify the brand. Ong Sau was a true connoisseur, a man of about fifty. He had an air of distinction about him that usually accompanies a man of achievement. It was evident from his surroundings and he loved his tea!

After a few exchanges of pleasantries, Tuyet came to the point. "I came here today because of my daughter. Her husband is already in America and she is still here with their three children. But she is living in a state of abuse by her mother-in-law who takes pleasure in tormenting her everyday – it's like torture living under that woman! I don't want to see my daughter lose the best years of her life under the control of that old hag. So I heard that you have some successful businesses, one of which I'd like to employ. Can you help me?"

Ong Sau was not a man to mince words. "First of all, it will cost you a lot, how many people are going to leave?"

"My daughter Thu Hoa and her three sons," she replied, "I would like to know when, where, and what time will the departure take place?"

"Well, your people could leave in two weeks, there are five seats left. But --- it will cost, I need five grams of 24 karat gold per person."

Perfect timing, Tuyet thought. She was excited, she had thirty grams of gold with her. "Just give me a deposit of half of the cost and you can give me the balance when your family completes the trip." He then added, "Give me your address and I will notify you three days before the boat leaves. What are your travel plans to reach the boat, can they be there within the three days?"

"My daughter will be sure of that. It will all go smoothly, the children will be ready."

"Very well, once under way, the trip will only take a week. The boat will leave Ho Chi Minh City and slowly make its way down the Saigon River until it reaches the last point of land on the left of the river called Vung Tau. It will then wait until the coast is clear of coast guard or possible pirates and then proceed out into the South China Sea. It will then head southwest along the Vietnam coast line until it reaches the southern tip of Vietnam at Nam Can. The same course will be maintained as it crosses the South China Sea toward Malaysia. The destination will be a refugee camp at the island of Pulau Bidong located off of the city of Kuala Terengganu on the Malay Peninsula."

Tuyet was quite happy for her daughter and grandchildren. Of course she was concerned about the safety and welfare of them on this trip, it could be dangerous. But she was reassured with the fact that members of Ong Sau's family would be going along also. So he wouldn't be someone that would cheat her out of the money. "Sounds good to me. Here's the ten grams of gold for half payment and I'll pay the rest at our final meeting."

He thanked her and smiled, "Everything will be allright. We are always very careful." While he was walking her out of the house, Tuyet started to weigh her decision against misfortune. Am I doing the right thing, she thought? Could I be sending my family to a death trap? I've got to follow through on this, life here is a living hell for them. All during the long walk back to Thu Hoa she remained preoccupied with her decision.

Upon reaching the house, she saw that her decision would indeed be correct, for the mother-in-law was sitting on the front porch howling at Thu Hoa while her daughter was combing her hair. Thu Hoa was somewhere inside the house. "Hello everyone," Tuyet cheerfully said, "I'm here to see my daughter and the grandchildren. Now that I have the chance while you're home, may I take them to my home for summer vacation? I'll bring them back in a month. That'll give us some nice time together."

Before she could answer, her daughter chimed in, "Mother, don't let the maid go away. I need her to wash my clothes and make breakfast for me. Let the kids leave but keep her."

"Sure you can take them," the mother-in-law replied, overriding her daughter's wishes, "but be back on time or I'll sic the dogs on you if you're late."

Goodness that was easy, Tuyet thought, no questions. It wasn't over yet though.

"Mother, why are you letting them leave? I need them here to wait on me."

"My pretty princess, they are poor people, they don't have enough money to feed themselves much less afford to help the rest of that family. Don't worry, they'll be back sooner than you think," she soothingly replied.

Tuyet entered and went back to the kitchen in the rear of the house. Thu Hoa was on her knees moping the floor. Her knees were bruised and the skin was raw and blood stained. "What happened to you Hoa?" Tuyet asked.

SOUTHEAST ASIA

Courtesy of the University of Texas Libraries, The University of Texas at Austin

"I just fell down and hurt myself, I'm fine." But Tuyet knew her daughter well. As a teenager, she was always well groomed – hair combed and set, face and body glowing, clothes immaculate. But now her hair was just tossed into a bun, her clothes were dirty and disarrayed, and her arms and legs were scarred up from the manual labor of cooking and cleaning.

Tuyet kept her emotions in check and said. "We have to leave now, it's two o'clock and we have to meet the bus." Thu Hoa had no idea what her mother had planned for her. So she packed lightly, three sets of clothes for her, and two sets of clothes for the each of the children. Being approximately the same height, the two younger boys could share with one another.

Thu Hoa and Tuyet gathered the belongings and went out of the front door to the porch. "Mother," Thu Hoa said, "I am leaving now to go to my mother's house for vacation. I'll be sure to be back at the end of the month. Take care of yourself and be sure to take your medicine – you have to be regular with that. If you get a letter from my husband, will you answer him and say that we miss him?"

"Oh dry up your crocodile tears! I'm not going to tell him anything, you pitiful person," the sister-in-law sneered. The mother-in-law smoothed over the rude remarks with her response, "Be good while you're away, I'll tell him that – have fun and come back soon."

While heading toward the bus station, Tuyet was now certain that she had done the right thing especially since learning that the relatives were keeping all communication away from Thu Hoa. She hadn't received or been allowed to read any letters from him since he left Saigon.

They caught a bus that was going southwest through town toward the Cho Lon area of the city. As it traveled down Tran Hung Dao boulevard, they enjoyed the many busy street scenes and places of interest. "Look, there's where all the Chinese medicine shops are, up on Trieu Quang Phuc street," Thu Hoa said. "Yes, I can smell all the herbs," Tuyet answered. "And there's the Tam Son Hoi Quan Pagoda, mother, dedicated to the Goddess of Fertility."

Tuyet smiled, "I don't need to visit there." They both laughed.

The Cholon long-distance bus station was very busy. They checked the schedule and found that their bus was a half hour late so they decided to walk two blocks down to the Binh Tay Market. It was easy to find, a yellow building with two wings and a tower at each end. A taller clock tower was in the center of the market. "Let's look at the imported Chinese toys mother, they're starting to bring them in again now that the border war is over. Maybe I can find something cheap to occupy the children on our long bus trip."

"All right, I'll look at their medicinal herbs," Tuyet said as she looked at her watch.

It wasn't long before they were on their way. They relaxed and pointed out places to the children as the bus traveled down Highway One. The countryside was pleasant and they passed many scenes of harvested rice lying on mats to dry out in the sun. My Tho was the first town to pass through and they noticed the many wooden boats and barges crowding the shores of the Mekong River as they traveled down the wide tree lined boulevards. The next town on the way was Vinh Long. Located on the Co Chien River, it was noted for beautiful orchards and gardens and many terrestrial orchids called "dia lan" were in bloom. They soon reached Can Tho and stopped for a rest break. This is the largest city in the delta and it serves as a transportation hub for the region in addition to being a major agricultural center. The passengers relaxed and watched the traders paddle from boat to boat along the floating markets in the Can Tho River. When the bus pulled out, the passengers all looked out the left side windows to enjoy the beautiful waterfront.

Soc Trang would be the last town before reaching Phu Loc. It is mainly noted for its festivals and religious sites. There are almost thirty Vietnamese pagodas in the town and surrounding areas. While riding through the district, Tuyet tells the children to watch for the college that she attended. "There it is, that's where I met your grandfather."

They arrived at Phu Loc around eleven o'clock and noticed a light in the window of their little makeshift house. My Lien opened the door when she heard a knock and shouted out loud to the children, "Grandma and Aunt Hoa are here, look at the children, all growing so big." To My Lien it was like magic having them home again. But it was the power of prayer, not magic, that fulfilled their hopes and dreams. The adults gathered around the dining table while the children played in the beds under the protection of the mosquito nets.

BINH TAY MARKET

Courtesy of Wikimedia Commons by author Lerdsuwa

Tuyet and My Lien talked to Thu Hoa about the escape plan because they sensed that she had felt some anxiety about the voyage. However, they soon rationalized that the only way to escape the control of her husband's family was to be reunited with him in America. And of course, there was the promise of a brighter future for her children.

The following days were happy ones. The children could play with their cousins while the adults could spend time together in the kitchen cooking and baking some goods to sell at the market. Everyone was content to be reunited again with their loved ones, a peaceful departure from the stressful times in their lives. But their living conditions made everyday family chores difficult. My Lien and Thu Hoa would have to go to the market place and buy wood for their small clay stove. Then they would cut the pieces into thirty inch lengths and split them up to make their cooking fires. Electricity and plumbing did not exist and routine chores required hard labor and ingenuity. To iron clothes for instance, a special iron had a place inside to hold a piece of burning charcoal that would heat the iron surface. Water had to be carried from a nearby stream or pond. So Tuyet and her daughters accepted these conditions in stride with the hope of a better future before them.

Then one day during the second week of the visit, a stranger passed by and gave Tuyet a note. She became excited and turned pale as he continued on without saying anything. "We better go inside the house," she said to her daughters, "leave the children here to play."

She opened the envelope and read – "The location is at the Saigon River near Thao Cam Park. Be there at 4am sharp three days from now. If you are late, we will leave without you. Bring dried food that will last for two weeks. We will provide water. Space is limited, pack light." Signed "Ong Sau"

———————————————————

"Well," Tuyet sighed, "the moment of truth is upon us. All good things must come to an end. We must start to prepare for Hoa's departure." At that, she packed her grandsons' clothing, then walked to the market for food. On the way she mumbled, I must select what would be best for the trip because space is limited to the bare essentials. Let's see, something sour instead of salty, that way they won't be as thirsty. Tamarinds will do it, the pods can be opened easily when ripe, and the pulp of the fruit is juicy. This "me" as we call it is good in vitamin B, calcium, and sugar even though it's acidic. What else? I'll make dried barbecue pork and some snacks for the children. Not too many – we don't want other people to notice.

The grandchildren were playing outside as she approached the front door. She hesitated and watched them play king and queen with crowns made from tree leaves. When they started to play with wet clay she entered the house with the sad thought that she will never see them play again.

There's always a busybody in the neighborhood and always at the most inappropriate time. "Hello neighbors! You sure have a lot of company. Are you having a party and not inviting me? Look at all this food."

"No party," Tuyet annoyingly replied, "I'm just making a nice meal for my kids before they have to leave for Saigon, Their vacation is almost over." Ignorance is bliss they say, and this bucktoothed woman proved it. She helped herself to the food and ate like a pig with no table manners. Everyone else moved away from the table as she dug into the food with her fingers.

The last day before any departure is always short. That night Tuyet spent some time with the visiting grandchildren reminding them to listen to their mother as she brushed their hair and prepared them for bed. "You need to be real good because you are going on a long trip," she whispered as she lied down on the bed beside them. "Now let me tell you a bedtime story."

A little while later Tuyet quietly left the bedroom and entered the kitchen. "Are the children asleep?" Thu Hoa asked. "Yes finally – they are excited!" My Lien then walked to the bedroom door to check on her children and found both of them asleep.

"All right, here's the plan," Tuyet began, "we will leave the house at four in the morning, that will put us in Saigon at nine in the evening. We'll stay at a motel and then head on over to the Saigon River at three am." No one spoke after that, reality set in and tears began to flow. Someone tried to cheer them up with a comment and laughter, then all became silent again. Everyone retired at midnight with the prospects of a new future, freedom, and the promise of being reunited.

All but Tuyet. She checked on the children to be sure that they were covered with the mosquito nets, the pests seemed to be more active than usual. She couldn't sleep so she prepared more food for the trip and set the breakfast table for the children. It wasn't long after that when it became time to get up. Thu Hoa was awakened but the children were difficult to get moving. It was now time to say goodbye to their cousins and aunts.

A few people were up and about outside. The usual nosy questions were asked, it looks like you all are leaving for a long time. Tuyet just smiled and guided her family toward the bus station. As before, she sat in the rear of the bus along with them and started to fall asleep as the vehicle began to move toward the highway.

They did make it to Saigon in good time, actually an hour earlier than predicted. Tuyet quickly instructed everyone on the way to be careful in the big city. "It's very crowded here, beggars lie on the side of the roads and pickpockets are already around here. I can almost pick them out. Watch your bags carefully and children, you hold on tight to us. Those people over there will kidnap you and sell you to the highest bidder to become beggers. They will break your arms and legs and make you cripple so that you can collect more money. They won't have any mercy and sometimes they won't even feed you. So always hold on to us. Watch where we're going." That was enough for them, the children held onto their grandmom's hands and their mother's pants legs while they walked toward the motel. After checking in, they dropped off their bags and went outside to a carry out cart and bought Pho Bo. As soon as they could, they returned to their room out of concern for their belongings.

The day of reckoning was here! "Wake up Hoa," Tuyet said as she tapped her on the shoulder. "We better get going, it's two am. Get the children up and be sure they stay quiet, we can't afford to be noticed." They quietly leave the motel and approached the three wheel vehicles that were waiting for fares. "It's thirty minutes to the river but we can't be dropped off there, it would be too noticeable," Tuyet whispers to Thu Hoa. "We'll hire the cab anyway and have him let us out a few blocks before the river."

Thirty minutes pass and they are still a good distance away from their destination. "This driver is taking us in a roundabout way to get more money, we better get out," Tuyet observes. "He seems half asleep mother, and I can smell alcohol. From the looks of him, he must have just been in a fight. Let's leave, we might not make it on time."

A few minutes later, they motion for the vehicle to stop at the bus stop near Thao Cam Park. While walking through the dimly lit path, they noticed other folks walking in the same direction, familiar faces but there were no greetings being shared. It seems like too many people Tuyet thought. She nudges Hoa and they walk faster to pass the crowd while carrying one child and almost dragging the others. "There's the boat mother and they're loading right now, hurry up!"

It was obvious that the boat was leaving sooner than scheduled. Thu Hoa and the children rushed on board. Tuyet didn't get to say goodbye to the grandchildren, she was distracted by Ong Sau. "I'll pay you the balance when I hear that my family has arrived safely," she said. Although the agreement was to make the final payment after the trip, Ong Sau seemed to be disappointed that the rest of the money was not paid now. There was no time to argue, the predawn sky was turning pink and sunrise would be minutes away.

Ong Sau shouted, "We have to leave now, we have no time to waste." The twenty-four- foot boat slowly pulled away from the landing while Tuyet waved from shore. She stood there and watched it sail away down the river. That's just an old fruit boat she thought, it wasn't meant to go to sea. Again the negative thoughts began to cloud her mind, did I do the right thing?

She sat down on a nearby park bench and started to cry, she felt weak, completely washed out. Then she began to pray, "Dear God and Lord of us all, please protect those innocent people. Dear Nhan, father of Hoa, watch over them. I will do anything to have you grant my wishes. Please bring them to safety."

It was time to go home. The sun was high and the day was hot. The city had come alive with crowds of people, streets full of all kinds of vehicles, pollution choked brown air, and standing room only on the city buses. Tuyet made her way back to the Cholon bus station and settled back on the bus for the long ride home. She arrived at Phu Loc around eight o'clock, just in time for dinner. As My Lien and her sisters gathered with the children around the table, the conversation was subdued. There was a feeling of emptiness about the departure of their loved ones.

Tuyet tried to stimulate the discussion, "My Lien, when are you going to see your husband?"

"I plan to go next week. I don't have enough money right now for the trip and all the food I'll need to bring. He uses everything so quickly, I prepare enough to last two months but lately he's been sharing it with his friends. It looks like I'll have to visit him more often."

"I'm very tired," Tuyet replied, "I need to go to bed. Let me sleep unless you hear something about Hoa."

Two weeks passed and not a word. Then out of the blue came Ong Sau. Tuyet wasn't home so he introduced himself to My Lien and the children. "Hello, I am Ong Sau, I have good news!"

"Come in, come in," My Lien excitedly replied. "Let me send the children to the market to get mother to come home." As she scurried Thao and Cungdiem out of the house, Ong Sau said that he needed the rest of the payment.

"Yes, as soon as Tuyet gets back. Tell me about the trip, I need to know all about it." She obviously wanted to take the trip herself with family, but not now, her husband was still captive in prison.

Tuyet quickly returned home with the children. Upon entering the house, she noticed that everyone including Ong Sau seemed to be very happy. Now my stomach feels better, it was full of butterflies – very nervous. "What are you doing here today Ong Sau? I didn't expect you so soon, I was going to come to Saigon to see you."

"They made it to Malaysia safely!" he beamed, "And I brought back a note for you."

"Dear Mother,

We made it here safely. It took a week and a half but we still have plenty of food and water. We miss you dearly, thank you for giving us a chance, you are my hero! Take care of yourself, I will write again soon.

Love, Hoa."

"It's her writing," Tuyet joyfully cries. She then went out to the rice field where the star fruit tree was located and retrieved the box. The last two bags of gold were removed and given to Ong Sau.

"Thank you so much for your service," Tuyet said, "If you plan another trip, let me know, I plan to have my other daughter leave too!"

CHAPTER 5

CAMBODIA

"An Overland Journey"

With the passing of a few years, things began to settle down except for my father who was still in prison. My aunts Thu Huong and My Lan had returned from hair dressing school in Saigon and were very successful. They started out in a shack with only a few customers but as time went by they became very popular with a large clientele.

I was now seven years old, old enough to realize the stress that my families had endured and the ongoing trauma that my mother My Lien faces everyday. And the pettiness of some of the people around town that were jealous of my aunts did not help the situation.

My mother had been faithful in her visits to the prison although the costs of her trips and support for her husband had prevented her from saving any money. She's scheduled to visit him again next week but a new crisis has arisen. The Communists keep coming to our little house and threaten to collect protection money. Mother is very upset over this harassment.

As usual, mother met with her friends and walked with them to the prison camp. But on her return I noticed that she was in tears. She didn't get to see father and they wouldn't tell her where he was now located. He had been transferred to another camp!

She dropped everything as she approached the house and hugged me. I wiped her tears away and stood there until she stopped crying. I didn't know what to say. When grandmother Tuyet came home she said, "What happened? Didn't you get to see him?"

"They transferred him somewhere mother and they won't tell me where he's been sent.I am so tired, I don't know how much longer I'm going to be able to cope with this miserable situation." My brother Thao and I just stayed quiet and out of the way. We went outside to play while grandmother tried to console my mother. A week passed by and still no news of my father Hieu.

Then one day around dinner time when everyone was home and we were preparing to eat a great meal for a change – fried fish, stewed pork, and steamed vegetables, I was asked to set glasses of water on the table for the adults. I looked out the window and saw a man walking toward the house. He looked like a down and out vagrant, he was dirty and his clothes were all torn. I ran to grandmother and told her. At that moment a knock on the door was heard and she answered it.

She was shocked! "It's Hieu! He's home! Come here Lien! It's your husband!" she shouts. My Lien dropped the rice bowl that she was passing around and ran toward her husband. "Thao, Cungdiem, come here. Your father is home!" I didn't know who my father was, I had no memory of ever seeing him. Thao later said that it had been a few years for him and he wasn't sure what father looked like. In spite of that we went to my father and he hugged us both. Then we went over to grandmother and held onto her legs. Father then removed his coat and sat down to eat. "I haven't had a meal like this in years. It is delicious. Oh how I missed your cooking."

"Tell us what happened," Tuyet asked, "My Lien went to see you and you were already gone. What about the other men, your friends?"

"Let him eat mother," My Lan said, "he's starving."

After dinner Thao and I cleaned the dishes then dutifully went to bed to allow the adults the freedom to speak frankly. Hieu told his story. "About two weeks ago, they concluded that they couldn't get any information from us so they decided to let us go. But we have to report to them once a month, if not, we'll be arrested again. That means that I'll have to go to Can Tho city where they're located. It's about a full day's travel by bus to get there."

My Lien became concerned. She thinks that it will cost all of her savings again to pay for his travel. And she knows his personality; in her mind she is sure that he values his friendships more than his family. It seems hard to accept that, she ponders, but the reality is that he can't stay settled in one place to build for the future. I hope I'm wrong.

In spite of her thoughts, Hieu was excited about being with his wife again and Tuyet notices the feeling of affection. She speaks up and says, "My Lien, you and Hieu go to your bed and bring Thao and Cungdiem to me. They can sleep with me from now on."

It wasn't more than two days later when Hieu decided that he wanted to visit his family in Saigon. My Lien was totally frustrated. She had been taking care of him all these years – traveling through the remote regions, saving money, paying off guards, providing food, and raising the children. And now he wants to visit family, people who didn't have the decency to come to Phu Loc to visit her and the children or to even ask about his welfare. But My Lien cannot make him stay home, he is the head of the family.

He did return shortly after and within a few months My Lien became pregnant with her third child. However, he would still be a vagabond and come and go as he pleased. Not for too long, he had to report to the Communists from his home address. But his concern for an income prompted him to try to start a business with his friends which required him to return to Saigon. He took My Lien's money and went his way while she still struggled to support her two children with a baby on the way.

The new school year brought some nice changes. Tuyet would teach with her grandchildren enrolled as students in her class. I loved it, I felt so comfortable yet I knew that I would have to perform well and get good grades so that I wouldn't embarrass my grandmother. And mother had her third child, another boy whom they would name Phuc. A nice looking baby brother with light skin and lots of hair.

Back to work though for My Lien, so Thao will have to take care of Phuc in the evenings. He didn't mind, he rather enjoyed it. It was 1985 and Thao was now ten years old. Being a very mature young boy, he took pleasure in bathing and feeding the infant. And at bedtime he would sing a lullaby for his little brother to put him to sleep. But every baby has some peculiar habit and Phuc was no exception. The child would munch on food while trying to sleep, especially dessert. Thao would have to go to the bakery store at all hours of the night if there was nothing at home to give to him. And he would cry until his demands were met.

When Thao and I would leave for school each morning, our youngest aunt, Thien Nga now sixteen, would take over the duties of caring for Phuc. Then after school, Thao would assume the responsibility. As any ten -year -old would do, Thao had his mishaps. While carrying Phuc on his back one day, he tried to jump over a ditch but tripped and fell in head first. He entered the house with the wet baby while soaking wet and smelling like some farm animal. Everyone was concerned about what happened and he told them after he cleaned himself. An embarrassing situation for a young boy that was trying to be responsible. But all in all, his devotion to family was most appreciated and they reassured him of that fact.

We did have fun though during those early days. I would go with Thao, and Phuc, to visit our neighbor who lived behind our house. The children all called him Ong Mien. He was half Cambodian and half Vietnamese with a very tall, thin and dark skinned physique. In spite of looking different, he allayed our fears by being good to us and his grandson was very funny to be around which gave us relief from the struggles that our family continually faced. So we spent a lot of time in their backyard picking mango and coconut to eat and playing house. We were very creative, everybody helped to gather leaves and branches from the trees that we would tie together to build a playhouse. We made a roof out of an old sheet with the leaves draped over the sheet. It would keep us happy while we enjoyed ourselves there, sometimes until dark.

Mother has two jobs now. During the day she sells pork at the market and then trims the fat for the customers. Thao collects the fat and brings it home to me to cut up in little pieces for the frying pan. The melted fat is saved and used as oil by mother when she fries cake to be taken to the movie theatre at night for sale to the patrons. I helped mother at the theatre while Thao took care of Phuc. During pleasant evenings, Thao will wash himself and Phuc, dress himself and Phuc up in their nicest clothes, and visit mother at the movie theatre. When the weather is bad, due to rain or high humidity, there will be no sales. So then I have to get up early and take the cakes to the market to sell and after a while that becomes a regular routine for me.

Father wasn't home much during these times. In fact, the only time he was home was when he ran out of money. He was always conjuring up dreams on how to make money for himself and My Lien. She got tired of hearing about these ideas that never seemed to work. And she was exhausted from taking care of three children while trying to keep body and soul together. I saw her cry a lot because of his lack of support for the family. I thought about getting work or creating some kind of business to help out. Something had to be done.

A few inquiries were made and I finally had a break. One of the neighbors offered me a job. It would be hard work but I didn't mind, after all I was now eight years old. I didn't want to struggle like mother for the rest of my life, I wanted to do better than that. Any experience would help I thought, so I accepted the job peeling shrimp at the Phu Loc Market. It was shrimp season and the company was busy exporting rice and frozen seafood.

I was paid by the pound of peeled shrimp and after a while I could peel them a lot faster and make more money. But the first day was terrible and discouraging. My fingers were cut and bleeding by the end of the day and there was even some swelling. I didn't want to tell my mom so I waited until everyone was asleep before I cleaned my hands and put on medicine.

Thao saw me with the medicine and tried to help me. I know he loved me and Phuc very much and still does, he has always comforted me and shown affection. I went on to save a lot of money; once I had two hundred dong and I opened a snack shack but being young, I ate up all the profits before the treats were sold. Oh well I thought, I'll try again. And I did a few months later. I found a job picking feathers off of chickens before they went to market.

Any time there was an occasion to attend a wedding, I did my best to be there. I particularly enjoyed the beautiful red and yellow gowns that were worn by the women. They were so attractive! One day I'll wear something just as beautiful.

That reminds me of my neighbor friends, they're twins, a girl and a boy.

Our culture says that twins have had past lives and their parents certainly believed that. And these twins must have promised each other to be together forever because when they are reincarnated, they will still be twins. Being fearful of that situation, their parents believed that the children may not survive. So the parents made a wedding announcement and invited all of the family and their many friends. But the bride and groom were life sized paper dolls. The wedding was a fabrication with gift offerings and prayers to their God. Afterward, they burned the dolls out of respect for their deity and to acknowledge the false wedding. Somehow this practice would permit the twins to lead a normal life. As bizarre as that may seem to the western world, some Asian people actually believed that it was necessary to perform this ritual to remove the perceived danger to the twins. But I digress, I must return to the story of my childhood.

I just wanted to have a normal life like all the other kids, kids who had the love of their fathers. When they would talk about doing things with their fathers, I couldn't recall anything that I had done with my father. And toys, I wanted a doll so bad but I couldn't get enough money together to buy one, so I collected some fabric and thread and made my own rag doll. My girl friends had pots and pans to play with, I gathered clay and formed it into pots and pans. When Thao and I would play fathers and mothers, I collected leaves and stitched them together to make a cape and hat for Thao and a gown for me.

The best times were had during the rainy season. After finishing our chores or on the weekends when we had more time, Thao and I would run down to the rice fields to catch soft shell crabs and snails. We had to watch out for the leeches though, I had one get on my big toe and I ran all the way home dragging my foot. Thao put a burning charcoal on the leech and it dropped off. Then he soaked my foot in salt water.

My Lien certainly saw the hard life that we were living in this dysfunctional family, and the poverty that existed both from the poor economy and the abusive treatment from the Communists. The future looked hopeless for the children. She decided to talk to Tuyet about their situation and their options to pursue a better life.

Just then Hieu returned home. So My Lien decided to prepare dinner instead and then after the children were in bed she would have a serious discussion with mother and Hieu. When the three of them were finally sitting around the dinner table alone, My Lien began. "Mother, you know how hard the children and I have to work every day. I don't want them to miss the opportunity to have a happy future. There's nothing here, and Hieu can't live here any more, he has to keep hiding from the Communists since he hasn't been reporting to them at Can Tho. I want to escape to America!!"

"Are you sure My Lien, it's dangerous?" Tuyet asked with an impending fear of losing her also. She realized that a plan to leave Vietnam would be in the best interest of all of her family but it was difficult to give up the close bond that had grown through the years of struggle. She shared a strong love with her daughters however, and that love would eventually influence her decision to continue the quest for their freedom. But not yet, please.

"We don't have any more gold right now and I don't know when Ong Sau will start another boat trip," she correctly admitted without suggesting that they pursue this issue further, more out of worry and fear then just not wanting to yield to their best interest. Sensing her deference to undertaking any venture at this time, Hieu offered an option, "I know another way, I know a lot of people who have successfully escaped by another way." Quickly My Lien responded, "Tell us how!"

"This is a journey across country, not by boat but on foot. We would go to Soc Trang and then to Can Tho on Highway One by bus. Then we would take Highway 91 by bus to Chau Doc close to the Cambodian border. That's a hundred miles from Soc Trang. We could afford the bus fare. Once over the border we follow the major highway on foot to Phnom Penh and then on to Battambang and the Thailand border. That's another three hundred miles. The Thailand government will take all refugees and help them to get to America. It will take about three weeks depending on weather and conditions, that's about fifteen miles a day. We'll cross the border at night and walk at night and sleep during the day."

Tuyet flinched at the thought of that long a distance on foot in a dangerous country. "I don't think that's a safe plan," she says, "Cambodian people don't have any mercy on outsiders, if they catch you crossing the border, they will cut your heads off and let the ants eat your bodies."

"Well, what choice do we have?" Hieu asks, "We have to try something!"

he emphasizes, probably out of fear of the Communists for violating his parole. "Look," he adds, "over 700,000 Vietnamese have been resettled in the United States already, the odds are in our favor."

While preparing to undertake the journey, Hieu decided to spend some time with the children before they left because the children would have to stay behind with their grandmother. It was a steady rain that morning but Hieu decided to take the children fishing anyway – it would be their last day together. He made a picnic basket for their lunch and packed the fishing net into the carrying bag. They walked down to the river in spite of the rain, it was just good to be doing something together at last.

I remember it well, watching father gather the net in his hands and casting it out over the water. It took some skill to have it billow out like some huge umbrella and then float down over the water. We called it "danh ca", fishing with net. The hardest part was the wait for ten minutes, Thao and I wanted to pull it in right away. Father was more patient and we spent the entire day there, casting the net and screaming with excitement when we saw something shiny near the top of the water. We didn't get a "mess of fish" as they say, only five little "ca", called tilapia.

I was glad to be back home that evening. It was dinner time and we were soaking wet. Mother helped grandmother set the table while we dried off and changed clothes. I could tell that grandmother Tuyet was very sad, mother and father will leave in the morning and it will be a long and dangerous trip.

Thao and I were also very sad. Our mother was leaving us with Tuyet but Phuc was going with her because she was still breast feeding him. Father stayed close to us until bed time that night then he told us a fairy tale until we fell asleep. It was one of my favorite stories. There were many Vietnam fairy tales, some gentle and others rather grim. "The Brocaded Slipper" is a story like Cinderella where she is mistreated by a cruel stepmother then discovered by a prince. "Little Finger of The Watermelon Patch" is like Thumbelina, the little girl lost in the forest who later becomes a queen. The themes of our stories can be seen in our literature, dances, and paintings. Fairy tales are very important in our culture, they imply a strong national unity and the children love to hear them.

My mother later told me that father went outside after he left us to enjoy the night air. It was so quiet that he could hear the hum of mosquitoes while he watched the lightning bugs fly over the nearby lake with their flickering lights reflecting off of the surface of the water. The star filled night sky was perfectly clear after the rains and the soft glow of lanterns added to the surrounding beauty.

My lien joined him a little later and he affectionately held her hands while he spoke. "I'm sorry that I haven't been a good husband to you and the children. Let me make it up by taking you on this journey to freedom. I made a wish that we would be safe without any problems as we travel. When we get to Thailand, we'll send for Thao and Cungdiem to come along. Don't worry, we'll get them there."

My Lien remained quiet while she rested her head on her husband's shoulder. She wanted to enjoy this tender moment, one of the few times that they could be peacefully together. Hieu felt a bit anxious though, he knew that the trip would be a challenge.

Tuyet was not one to be overwhelmed by sorrow. She awakened early as usual and prepared to leave for the bakery before the others were out of bed. She covered her head with her special blue scarf with the red and yellow criss-crossed stripe pattern – a favorite among Vietnamese women. When she arrived back at the house with bread for Hieu and My Lien, she noticed that their bags were already at the door. "We're ready to go mother," Hieu announces, "thank you so much for all of your help this past year, My Lien and the children appreciate it. I hope you don't mind too much about keeping Thao and Cungdiem, as soon as we get there we'll send you a letter."

After they hug Tuyet, she removes her scarf and puts it around Phuc. A snack for the baby is then placed in one of the bags. Slowly they depart, Hieu is carrying the bags while My Lien walks beside him carrying the baby. They stop some distance away, turn around, and wave. Soon they are out of sight while Tuyet squints her eyes to hold back the tears. After a long pause she enters the children's room and gives them a kiss on the cheek while she pulls up the blanket and lies down beside them. They're still asleep.

I had an empty feeling when I got up to go to school. My mother was gone and grandmother must have noticed my lethargy, she did her best to be cheerful to Thao and me. Being in grandmother's class was helpful, we would get to be with her all day, from the time we left home together to the recess in the teacher's breakroom. We also shared lunch and when the bell rang for dismissal, we walked home singing all the way. Grandmother Tuyet loved to hear me and Thao sing and we had many happy times after school. The evenings were also fun. Once in a while I would help my aunts prepare wigs for brides since their hair salon business was doing very well with lots of customers.

———————————————

Time passed quickly and at the end of three weeks we hadn't heard about my parents or received a letter. Since it would take three weeks to get to Thailand, grandmother Tuyet decided to wait a bit longer. More time passed and Tuyet became quite nervous and anxious. Her husband's tragedy keep haunting her and filling her with dread over the whereabouts of her daughter and son-in-law. Sometimes she felt as if she were numb and out of control.

I can't wait any longer, Tuyet thought. My nerves are going to make me sick if I don't do something. So she took the Saigon bus once again to try to see if her family had been arrested while trying to cross the border. Friends and relatives were contacted to learn about any refugees or travelers that had been taken into custody. She even went to the local Communist government office for information about prisoners but learned nothing. They did say that she could contact the prison at Nha Trang in South Central Vietnam for information.

Another two hundred miles. I'll have to do it! Route One will follow the coast northward, the scenery should be enjoyable. It wasn't long before the bus passed Ta Cu mountain. Tuyet could see the cable car that carried tourists up the 2100 foot hillside to the one hundred and sixty foot white Reclining Buddha, the largest in Vietnam.

Several hours later the bus reached Phan Rang Thap Cham city and they stopped for a rest at the well preserved Cham Towers, twin religious brick towers built in the 13th century.

She finally arrived at Nha Trang, Vietnam's famous beach resort where the mountains reach down to dark green palm trees that face the brilliant white sands along the coastal blue waters. It is also home of the Long Son Pagoda dedicated to the numerous Buddhist monks who were killed or died protesting the corrupt Diem regime. Tuyet hailed a rickshaw and rode to the local prison. She was informed that some people had been recently arrested and imprisoned near the Laotian border. Upon leaving the prison office, she inquired further with some of the local neighbors. They confirmed the official statement and added that the arrests had been made about two weeks ago.

The towns closest to the southern Laotian border were Plei Kan and Dak Glei. Another long bus ride but she was determined. This time she would take Route 26 to Buon Ma Thuot, Vietnam's coffee capital in the Central Highlands, then north on Route 14 to Kontum city. She enjoyed the mountainous view of the thriving coffee plantations but the terrain around Kontum Province stood out in stark reality with its numerous bomb craters from the war. They passed several villages with wooden stilt houses where the walls and roofs were covered by dried branches of leaves. There were also the elaborately carved "long houses". They were the homes of the Degar hill tribe known to their American Green Beret allies as "Montagnards". These tough mountain fighters had suffered decades of persecution by the Communists and thousands of them were still in prisons for having met the Viet Cong on equal terms.

Tuyet decided to rest for the night in Kontum. She would get a fresh start in the morning after inquiry about the location of any prisons near the Laotian border. As good luck would have it, the only prisons in the area were at Dak Glei and Kontum. Dak Glei was located right on the Laotian border about 100 miles due north. That had to be it. Before she left though, she visited Kontum prison to be sure. On the way she passed the impressive all wooden Catholic Church that the French had built – another example of the numerous attempts at French colonization.

She had her choice to use the same long distance carrier to continue up Route 14 or to take passage on a local and cheaper bus. Upon inquiry, she found out that the local buses raced down the mountain sides to be the first to collect passengers and fare. My nerves are bad enough she thought, I'll pay the extra fare.

The northern swing through Kontum Province had its own charm. They passed the highest granite mountain in the area at a height of 2600 meters. Fifty percent of the land was forest with 26,000 ha, or 64,246 acres available for cattle grasslands. The dark volcanic Basalt soil was perfect for the rubber and coffee plantations. Tea and sugar cane farms were also passed.

At last she was there - Dak Glei! The prison looked more like a storage warehouse with run down shacks scattered about it, all surrounded by barb wire fences. There were a few people milling around, hardly any children but then she heard a baby cry, a familiar cry. Could it be? She forced herself to approach the dreaded guards to ask if she could see the people in one of the shacks. Of course they refused, it was the same old badger game of extorting money from visitors. Immediately she pulled out some cash and the now wide-eyed guards opened the gate.

She cautiously walked up to a darkened door entrance and looked inside. The shock unsettled her so much that she lost her balance – it was My Lien! Her baby Phuc was feverish and covered with a rash. Tuyet had to get them out of there. With tears running down her cheek, she pleaded with the officer, "Please sir, my daughter is here and she made a big mistake. She ran away with her boyfriend and their child. It's my grandson and he is very ill. I need to get him to a doctor or he will die, please sir, please I beg you." Tuyet had to be extremely cautious about identifying her family. She couldn't say that the man was My Lien's husband, they would determine that he was Hieu Tang, wanted for parole violation.

When she finally fell to her knees to plead once more, the officer threw up his hands and left. While he was gone, Tuyet hugged My Lien and Hieu and asked about Phuc. Before they could answer the officer was back. He couldn't have been gone more than ten minutes. "Give me all your money," he said, "and I'll let them go." Tuyet quickly reached into her hidden pocket and pulled out some folding money. Her reaction was fast enough for the officer to assume that this was all she had. Yet she needed money to get home so there was still another clip of money in the pocket – a well thought out plan in anticipation of the guard's demands. "Thank you sir, I will teach my daughter a lesson when she gets home and I'll take care of this troublemaker also!" she emphasized while pointing an accusing finger at Hieu. "Let these people out," the officer said and the barb wire gate at the entrance was opened. They quickly walked through the opening into the heavily forested Bolaven Plateau that extended down from the eastern slopes of Laos. Were it not for their circumstances, they would have enjoyed the Laotian side of the border with its 100 foot high waterfalls and the Nang Fa crater lake, a virgin lake with sky blue water surrounded by peaks of mountains.

They walked as fast as they could along the dirt road toward town. The abundant wildlife could be heard along the way, an occasional Asian elephant crashing through the underbrush or the roar of a black bear while overhead flew the popular Ibis. Soon they reached the outskirts of Dak Glei, and they had to hurry – Phuc's fever seemed to be getting worse!

There was a small hospital close by so they entered and requested to see a nurse. What little money they had left could not be spared for a doctor. One of the nurses in attendance volunteered to take a look at Phuc. She placed an ice pack on his head and gave him some cold medicine. After waiting a few hours, they noticed that his fever had started to recede. It would now be time to leave to get away from this area as soon as possible.

They made their connections at the terminal and waited for departure time. Once the bus was boarded and everyone was settled, Tuyet had to ask, " What happened, what went wrong?"

"Well, the first week went very well," Hieu admitted, "we made it to Chau Doc by bus and began to walk toward the border. Our destination was the town of Takeo in the Takeo Province on the Cambodian side of the border."

"We did feel comfortable as we passed the small villages with their stilted huts because the local Cambodians were Khmer people, some of their group actually lived around us, as you know, in the Mekong Delta. They practiced a combination of Buddhism, Hinduism, and ancestor worship, similar to our beliefs. So we had a kindred spirit with these rice farmers and fishermen and their Khmer Krom language could be understood somewhat from exposure to it back home.

"We traveled up the Mekong River floodplain between the Bassac and Mekong Rivers until we reached Takeo. The Khmers warned us of the locations of minefields and unexploded ordnances that still existed and the many bomb craters from the saturation bombing in the region around the Ho Chi Minh Trail. Another concern was the impact of the Khmer Rouge under Pol Pot. They almost destroyed the culture of the people until the Vietnamese Army drove them out. But they still control areas in western and northern Cambodia. You're right Tuyet, we would have had to avoid these people.

CAMBODIA

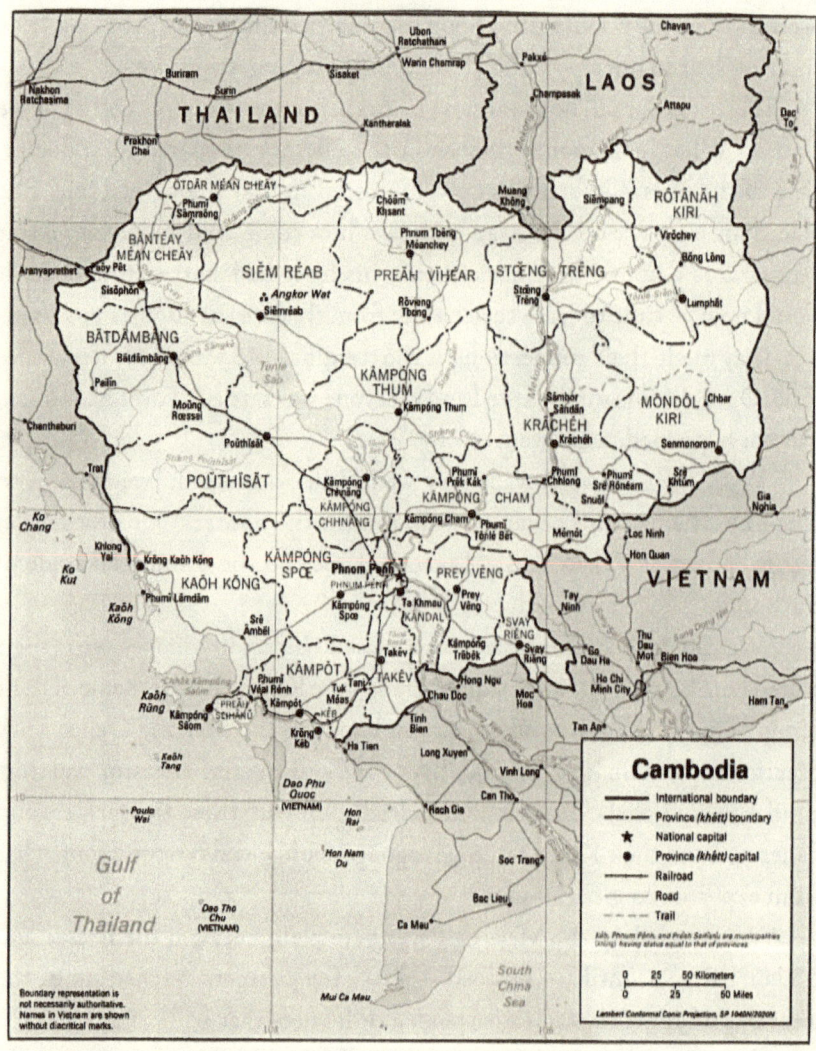

Courtesy of the University of Texas Libraries, The University of Texas at Austin

88

ROYAL PALACE IN PHNOM PENH

Courtesy of The CIA World Factbook

"The villages around Takeo were mostly occupied by the famous silk weavers and a few miles north of Takeo was Phnom Chisor mountain. We climbed the five hundred steps to get a view of the terrain to better plan our route and then we surprisingly saw temple ruins from the tenth century. After that we headed east to the river and learned that many large wooden boats delivered cargos from Vietnam.

"Our plan was to catch a ride from Phnom Penh to Siem Reap town on the Tonie Sap Lake. This would put us in the Siem Reap Province on the Thailand border. But the boats were being watched for illegal immigrants so we decided to walk to the next province north of Phnom Penh, the city they once called the Pearl of Asia, and board a boat when it stopped halfway up the lake at Kampong Chhnang.

"That's when things began to come apart while we were on our way to Phnom Penh. We came upon a group of travelers and journeyed together for awhile. To the west in the distance were the forested mountains but to the east was the ever-wet heart of Cambodia. Then one day we encountered a patrol while passing through a forested jungle. We could hear the dogs barking in the distance. The sounds kept getting closer as they must have picked up our scent. Everyone ran and spread out in different directions while we continued north. My Lien soon tripped and hurt her ankle. She had protected Phuc as she fell so she couldn't avoid the injury. She limped along in pain until I saw that further attempts to escape were useless. The army patrol caught up as the snarling dogs surrounded us. We stood perfectly still, huddled together while holding Phuc between us. I could feel the tremor in My Lien's arms but the dogs did not attack. We admitted to the patrol that we were Vietnamese so the officer said that they would carry us to our authorities.

"After traveling a great distance while under guard, we wound up at Dak Glei where we were turned over to our Vietnamese captors. The Laotian police worked well with the Cambodian authorities and they had mutually agreed to return us to our native soil for further disposition."

"Then what happened to my grandson, why was he so sick?" Tuyet queried, obviously upset.

My Lien sighed and responded, "While we were imprisoned they didn't feed us, so we were nearly starving, which kept me from having enough breast milk for Phuc. To make matters worse, mosquitoes and bugs would bite us all night long and poor Phuc had lots of caterpillars crawling over him in the dark. It was so dark, I could hear him crying but I couldn't tell what was happening. Finally, two days ago, I borrowed an oil lamp from some of the women, that's when I saw the ants and caterpillars on him." Tuyet didn't respond, she was devastated. She stayed quiet for the rest of the trip but kept thinking about how to get My Lien and her family to leave the country by sea.

At last, Phu Loc, what a relief for the exhausted travelers. While walking to their home, the usual nosy neighbors peered out of their windows or walked by the family. Some even sent their children to find out what had happened. It wasn't more than one week after their return from the aborted effort to escape that Hieu decided to visit his relatives. My Lien was furious, he just won't stay in one place and try to support his family.

She had to put him out of her mind and focus on earning a living again. This time she would work as hard as possible to save enough money to leave Vietnam and to keep that money hidden until then. The stress was beginning to take its toll. She was becoming upset more often and demanding more discipline from her children. Unfortunately, her bottled up anger was being directed to Thao and Cungdiem and she became physical with them with frequent beatings.

Yes, she did take her anger out on us and it was a very difficult and sad time. I loved my mother very much and was hurt more by her unhappiness than the punishment I received. I was old enough to understand her pain so I tried to look beyond those outbursts.

Tuyet also noticed the unusual treatment, she didn't like it but she understood the situation and with her protective insight she knew that she had to do something. So off she went, once again, for a scheduled visit to Ong Sau in Saigon. This time as she approached his house she noticed several men loitering around the premises, trying to be casual and unnoticed. But she knew that they were most likely Communists and that they were watching his house. I better keep my distance she thought, so she walked away and headed toward Van Hoa Park, two blocks away. "What am I going to do now," she unconsciously said out loud while sitting down on a park bench. But suddenly an old man walked up without paying any attention to her and sat down. He secretly handed her a note, hesitated for a few minutes, got up, and walked away.

She looked around slowly to see if he had been followed. Then she opened the note and quickly glanced down while avoiding the appearance of reading something. It read, "Meet me like we did before to discuss matters. This time at Rach Gia Bay – you will be informed of the address. Be there at three o'clock sharp!"

―――――――――――――――――――――

―――――――――――――――――――――

CHAPTER 6

RACH GIA BAY

"The Unforgiving Sea"

The trip from Phu Loc to Rach Gia Bay would be routine for the most part, especially with the amount of traveling that Tuyet had seen over the last few years. But once she reached Long Xuyen about thirty miles northwest of Can Tho, the remainder of the trip would be slow and dusty with heavy traffic flowing southwest down route 80, a minor road that led to the port town of Rach Gia.

Tuyet had departed early from home that day in case of traffic congestion or delays in the bus schedule. She was content with making this travel precaution, it would allow her time to review all of her concerns and prepare a list of questions regarding the well being of her family. And with the history of recent events, her own peace of mind was important too!

The beautiful blue waters of the Gulf of Thailand were strangely placid to Tuyet as compared to the rough surf back home in the South China Sea. Tuyet stood along side the statue of Nguyen Trung Truc in the center of Rach Gia city and scanned the urban sprawl of the busy town that sat on a small island in the Cai Long River. The north and south branches of the river flowed around the island into Rach Gia Bay that served as an estuary for the Gulf.

She decided to visit the Truc Temple before moving along to the meeting place. The national hero there was a young twenty-two year old swashbuckler who captured Rach Gia from the French and destroyed a ship of their line back in 1861. He was later executed by them at the Rach Gia market square after being captured on Phu Quoc island that was located some fifty miles offshore in the Gulf of Thailand.

There wouldn't be time to visit the ancient city of Oc Eo where ruins and artifacts had been found. She decided to someday visit the much more elaborate excavations at My Son in Central Vietnam near Da Nang. Traces of nearly seventy temples could be seen there, existing since the 4th century. But Oc Eo was the more interesting place to her because of the Funan Kingdom influence dating back to the first century when it was introduced to Vietnam by India in spite of the Chinese settlements and culture that dominated the region.

Tuyet soon became distracted from her historical pondering when she noticed the busy activity along the river. People were fishing while others were selling fruits from their boats. Upon reaching the shore of the bay, children could be seen swimming near houseboats while other people were rowing their small boats across the river.

It felt good to sit down and enjoy a sugar cane drink with her Banh Mi, and the sun was bright and clear with just enough breeze to be comfortable. But time was moving along, it was three-twenty. Am I at the wrong place, she anxiously thought. As she got up to stretch her legs and look around, a pleasant voice asked, "What can I do for you?" It was Ong Sau, he had already been there but remained distant until satisfied that the area was safe.

"Oh, hello, I was afraid that I missed you," Tuyet excitedly replied. "Are you going to plan another trip soon? I am desperate to have my other daughter and her husband leave the country," she added.

"Well, we plan another trip in early spring, in March actually. How many people will join us?"

"There will only be two adults," Tuyet replied while mentally assuming that she would keep the children until My Lien and Hieu become established.

"Then I will need four bags of gold, 5 grams in each bag. You can pay me half like before and the balance after they arrive safely."

"But this is twice what you charged before!"

"It is more difficult now," he admonished. "We can't leave Saigon like the last time. And our meetings have to be in remote places so the expenses are much higher. The government is watching for illegal emigrations with more resources now in the police and coast guard, so our effort to provide a safe journey is becoming more difficult."

On that note Ong Sau abruptly stood up and departed. As he walked away, Tuyet felt excited about the opportunity but also concerned and worried about the large outlay of gold that is now required. I don't have much time to collect the money needed, it's already February, she thought. She remained seated on the bench, transfixed on the nearby scene of happy children swimming in the bay as she recalled all of the ways that she could raise money and whether there would be time enough to meet his demand. Needless to say, she was totally preoccupied on the trip back to Phu Loc.

Regardless of the circumstances, the return home was always a pleasure. Tuyet's daughters were cheerful as usual when she arrived, with laughter ringing throughout their humble house. And the children seemed content and secure in the presence of My Lien and their loving aunts. Tuyet felt fortunate to have such a strong and supportive family in spite of the hardships they faced on a daily basis.

I dread the thought of disturbing this tranquil scene, why can't we just stay in the moment forever? But she knew it was not to be – it was time for another part of the family to fulfill the dream of reaching a new life and freedom.

"Girls, I need to talk to you after dinner, get the children to bed early," she whispered.

It was late in the evening when My Lien, My Lan, Thu Huong, and Tuyet finally got together around their small round kitchen table. Tuyet talked in hushed tones about the forthcoming trip but her youngest daughter Thien Nga, now almost seventeen years old, was eavesdropping on the conversation behind the door. She had been aware of the plans and was determined to leave with My Lien. Tuyet would forbid such a departure and Nga knew it, so she quietly slipped into bed and pretended to be asleep.

Hieu came home the next day from another of his numerous trips. My Lien immediately explained to him about the new opportunity. He didn't seem to be too impressed with the proposal as he continued to play with the children. "Let's wait for your mother to come home from work and then we'll discuss it further," he murmured.

My Lien just shrugged and entered the kitchen. She grabbed a straw shopping bag and left for the market – not that her dismay would be relieved there, there would be many questions about her recent absence and they would all be given a curt answer, "I was spending time with my in-laws in Saigon." And that was it!

Maybe a good cup of "chau ga" will cheer me up, she thought. So she purchased some chicken and vegetables and headed home. On the way she met Tuyet coming from work. Good, now I can cook dinner right away.

The delicious smell of the broth made everyone hungry; they all helped to prepare for this favorite meal. Hieu washed the children, Nga laid out the spoons and chopsticks, and the rest of the family sat down at the table. It was delicious! Everyone ate at least two bowls of the soup. Soon it was the children's bedtime and Tuyet was anxious to get down to business. "Hieu and My Lien, listen to me carefully. I want you to take the gold I've saved and go to Saigon to see Ong Sau. The boat trip is planned for early March and I trust him completely. He took your sister and her children safely to Malaysia, and he got them there in plenty of time. I want you people to have a better future and once you get settled, you can send for your children or My Lien can come back for them. In the meantime, I will take care of them. Thao is older, he can help me. Diem can help around the house, and Phuc is still too little to travel - I remember well how sick he was after your last attempt to leave." They called her Diem now instead of Cungdiem, a nickname.

My Lien appeared hesitant, uncertain about leaving her children behind but she said nothing. Hieu was quiet for a time while Tuyet waited for a response. Finally he said, "Mother, may I speak for the family?" Tuyet raised her head in agreement and listened. He paused again, then said, "I will only go if my family goes with me – My Lien and the children. If we are killed, we will all die together. You've been a great role model for us, you are a wonderful mother-in-law – more than I could have ever asked for. But the last time we tried to leave, our children were left behind. We feel that we need to stay together, all of us. My Lien and I are willing to take the risk and I hope that you will honor that."

Tuyet looked at her family, then squinted her eyes to stem the flow of tears. "Very well," she uttered, "It's your decision as adults and parents. Let's plan to get ready, early March will soon be here."

Everything seemed to be settled until a loud footstep was heard entering the kitchen. It was Nga. "Mother, I want to go too! I don't want to live here anymore. I hate it here. I want a different life too!" she shouted. Everyone was shocked at the aggressive behavior of the teenager. It was totally out of character. Tuyet composed herself and calmly said, "No, you are not going anywhere. You are to stay here, finish college, and be a teacher like me. You will also be a big help to your sisters." Nga slowly turned and left the room. They could all hear her quietly sobbing through the night.

The seriousness of her complaint would not be realized until the following evening. Nga had left the house early and crossed the rice field to the star fruit tree. She sat there all day with her favorite book and refused to take her meals – it was a hunger strike to protest against her mother's demands.

I remember it well, the early spring weather was beautiful with clear fresh air gently blowing across the fields. Grandmother sent me to the rice field with food and drink for aunt Nga. I skipped and sang all the way while carrying my bucket. She had fallen asleep so I shouted, "Aunty, wake up, grandma sends you some food." Nga started to stir and I said, "Do you want to eat, if you don't I'll eat it, the cake is still warm and it smells so good!" The sweet smell of coconut and vanilla carried across the breeze to both of us and I could hear her stomach grumble. "No," Nga emphatically answered, "Take it back home, I'm not eating until mother lets me go with you."

What was I to do, I was a little kid? So I sat quietly next to Aunt Nga and waited. And the longer I waited, the more hungry I got, the warm food made my mouth water. Finally I said, "All right, I'll take the food back to grandma but it won't be there when you decide to eat."

I now knew something was wrong and I became scared. After running as hard as I could, I rushed into the kitchen and yelled, "Grandma, Aunt Nga looks sick, she can't lift her hand to hold the cake. I tried to give her some. You've got to do something! You've got to do something!" And I jumped up and down and pointed to the fields.

Tuyet quickly took some cake and water and rushed to the star fruit tree. She looked all around and across the rice field – Nga wasn't there! Now she was really worried. There was an old shack nearby so Tuyet decided to look inside. There was Nga lying down on the floor in a fetal position, holding her stomach. Tuyet was desperate. "All right, I'll let you go, under one condition, you'll have to listen to your sister and her husband. You are my baby daughter and I don't want you to leave me." Nga sat up and smiled. She gulped down the cake while they walked home together. Tuyet wasn't giving up yet but she had to do something.

"Beware the ides of March," was a warning to Julius Caesar and it was also true in this case. The family was making final preparations for their exodus but caution would be necessary. They had to be very discreet in their activities or one simple mistake would result in the arrest of everyone. The Communists were on alert and they seemed to be watching for suspicious behavior on every corner.

The last dinner together had been carefully prepared. It was "déjà vu" - Tuyet recalled the same scene with Thu Hoa and her children and now she had to endure it again. She immersed herself into the preparation and made "canh chua", a hot and sour soup. For the main course, she served "ca chien", fried fish and sauce, and "thit kho", a pork dish. Everyone enjoyed the meal or pretended to do so; laughter and tears were shared until finally everyone became quiet. Tuyet broke the silence to say, "All right, we have an early trip tomorrow, let's clean up and set the bags aside to be ready. We'll each carry one bag and some of the dried food for the journey."

The bright moon glow made silhouettes of the buildings and roadway, just enough to allow the anxious travelers to easily wend their way to the bus station. Not many people were waiting for departures at this early hour, so they entered the near empty bus and hurried to the rear seats as Tuyet had done before. The bags were placed under the seats to be carefully protected with their feet.

I insisted on sitting next to my father but fell asleep as soon as the bus left the terminal. Thao tried to stay awake so that he could watch the road and scenery – it was his first venture away from home. He lowered the window slightly to enjoy the beauty of the countryside that was protected by their God, Tan Vien. Soon enough the wind against his face tired him out and he rested. At each bus stop, vendors would run forward and try to sell snacks. The noise and excitement awakened both children and they would sometimes be given a treat – cold and sweet sugar cane soaked in ice for Diem, and a bag of Mango slices for Thao.

I had never seen anything as beautiful as Saigon at night. There were so many lights, vehicles and buildings, especially the buildings with accent lighting to highlight a façade or a roof line. The streets were jammed with cars and motorbikes, weaving in and out of traffic with two riders on the bikes. I kept tugging at Thao's arm while shouting to look at everything at once. There were plenty of street vendors with well lit tents to display clothing on racks or food being prepared by cooks wearing chef's hats and aprons.

After a while, we checked in to the motel then left to get dinner from a street stall. Grandmother had done this before and she wanted to conserve money. Mother seemed to be very happy, she was with her husband and children and I heard her say, "Tomorrow we will be on our way to freedom and our dream." My father put his arm around mother and smiled.

Grandmother and Aunt Nga sat beside me at the low table on some small stools while we ate dinner and looked at the passing parade. The street was filled with beautiful people walking up and down past the displays. One group of women wore white conical hats yet each was dressed in a different colored "Ao dai" – white, green, purple, and orange. It sure was different from our little town. We walked for awhile after that, then returned to the motel. Some of Ong Sau's people were waiting for us. They handed grandmother a note and disappeared in the blink of an eye.

Mister Ong Sau was sure right about the remoteness of the meeting place. We had to go all the way over to the mountains near Chau Doc. That was close to the Cambodian border where my mother and father started their walk to escape. And to meet at the Quan Am thien tu temple way back in the forest was not going to be easy.

But we took the three hour bus ride to Chau Doc city and then began our walk up Sam Mountain to the temple. There were shrines, grottos, pagodas, and ancient tombs all over the place. At last we reached the temple and there it was – an imposing statue of the Chinese Goddess of Mercy, Quan Am. She was clothed in an all white gown with her arm slightly elevated in greeting. The temple was very old, just a rundown big house without any caretakers. But Quan Am seemed to be very popular, there is a statue of her in the center of Chau Doc.

Grandmother said that it was a good omen! She and Thu Hoa had passed a Quan Am pagoda on the way to the Cho Lon bus station in Saigon. It was on a side street off of Tran Hung Dao Boulevard, one block from the Goddess of Fertility pagoda. Thu Hoa had a good trip, so we should also be fortunate.

We walked toward the temple and were met by a Buddhist nun, a Su Co, who directed us to the guest room in the rear of the temple. Some folks were already there, very affluent, from their clothing styles and display of jewelry. They kept to themselves while the Su Co brought out water and snacks for the children.

She then went outside to greet about fifty-five people. Once they were settled, Ong Sau entered with two men. "Hello everyone," he said, "thanks for arriving on time, here are my best captains, they will navigate and take the boat to Thailand. All the details will be explained later. Any questions?"

Ong Sau then sat down and the two men began to talk and answer questions. Everyone was captivated and concentrated on the speakers. They absorbed every detail. Then Ong Sau stood up and said, "The journey will begin a week from today. We will meet here once again for a final session before departure."

As they departed the temple, Tuyet thought about the possibility of strangers in the area being noticed and confronted. She and her family would stand out in this border town centered on water. Saigon was a bustling metropolis where they could get lost in the crowds. So she decided to take the family to visit and stay with relatives in Long Xuyen.

It was a happy reunion, the relatives were glad to see everyone again. I enjoyed it especially – the house was on water! There were two kinds of these houses, stilt and floating. Floating houses could move downstream to better business opportunities. Some people live their entire lives on these houses, rarely setting foot on dry land. They even have gardens and animals. But the house we were visiting was on poles. There were cracks between each piece of floorboard so Thao and I could look down and watch the waves hit the poles. I loved it there! At night we could watch the fish jumping out of the water for air and the breezes were so fresh in spite of the burning oil lamp to ward off mosquitos. Our hosts were very kind, they fed us and gave us our favorite dessert, "Che soi nuoc", a rice ball pudding. They were so large that we could only eat half of the bowl. In the evenings, the adults would go outside to the back of the house and talk while we children went to bed.

An interesting feature of the floating houses were the fish traps suspended below a trap door in the floor. They would catch fish in the woven bamboo nets whether the house was still or moving down the river. Most of the houses had pitched roofs and windows while some of the poor people lived in floating shacks. Both types of houses were connected to shore by monkey bridges – which I love to cross!

It wasn't more than two days later that some of Ong Sau's people approached us near the market and announced that the boat is nearby – in Long Xuyen!

"How did they find us so easy?" Nga exclaimed.

"People in this kind of business must be very powerful because they have a lot of people working for them and a lot of connections," Tuyet replied. One of the men then said, "Ong Sau sent a message – meet him at the boat that has a red scarf tied on top of the roof."

The excited wayfarers quickly walked toward the market and looked for the boat. My Lien, Nga and the children stayed at the market while Tuyet and Hieu continued the search. They finally found it about three miles upriver toward Chau Doc. It was a typical vegetable boat, about twenty-four feet long with high wooden sides and several windows. The sides curved around and upward toward the bow. At the top of the pointed bow was a flat surface that permitted the boat to butt up against a pier. There were many of these boats scattered around the river in this floating market with a variety of fruits and vegetables. Their boat was tied up at a landing and a woman was casually standing beside it. Tuyet asked, "Excuse me miss, are you selling any fruit today?"

"Yes, come on board and take a look at our Jack fruits, they're all ripe and smell good."

They climbed aboard and saw Ong Sau sitting in the stern, relaxing with a cup of his favorite tea. Tuyet thought, he amazes me with his huge communication webb yet he always seems so nonchalant and unassuming.

"Sit down folks, we've got a lot to discuss," he cheerfully said. Then he motioned for the attendant woman to lower the curtains so people outside could not see the conversation take place.

"I have bad news and good news! The bad news is - we lost our captain and navigator. The good news is – I still plan the trip. It's too late to turn back, all the passengers have arrived and paid their fare.

Tuyet started to get excited but he interrupted her and said, "I want to renegotiate our deal. I know Hieu was in the military and you know where you want to go. And your brother-in-law Nam was also in the military. So you two men take over command of the boat. I wont charge the rest of the gold if you decide to take responsibility."

Well now Tuyet was really apprehensive. She weighed the pros and cons in her mind. Will Hieu and Nam learn how to read charts, navigate, operate the engine, and maintain discipline? Everything is ready to go in less than a week, can they learn that fast? They've been trained in the military to handle stressful situations though. She settled down and began to ask an essential question. "Why did you wait until the last minute to tell us this? There are many lives on this boat, I don't know if my family is capable of being responsible for them."

Hieu reacted immediately, "We can do this mother! My brother-in-law and I can do it together. We've been through training before, we'll learn everything in the next few days." Ong Sau then motioned for the attendant to bring in one of his employees. "This is Xuan," he said, "he can teach you the basics about the boat and the engine, just be sure to take notes and practice." As an afterthought he added, "When you're ready, you'll depart from Rach Gia Bay at three in the morning, no later! This will be the boat that's going out to sea." Ong Sau then left Hieu, Nam , and Xuan to explore the workings of their craft while Tuyet departed and rejoined her family with the breaking news.

A quick inspection by Hieu caused him to be concerned about the safety of the trip. It was a fairly small wooden boat used primarily to shuttle fruit and rice across the river. The cabin wasn't much more than a large wooden hood with windows. Comfort was out of the question, there were no rooms or bathrooms, only a small box cubicle setting beside the engine. He rationalized the situation by saying that no matter what we do, if our

God decides to take us, it will be His will. So we will place our faith in God's providence and hope that He will protect us.

Hieu then returned to the guest house where his family and relatives had been greeting more arrivals for the voyage. Two young, single men were introduced, Nghia and Loc. They would become friends with Hieu and Nam and become valuable assets on the trip. They quickly learned how to operate the engine and handle the sail so that duties could be shared among the men.

On their final day in Long Xuyen, Tuyet made an effort to convince Nga to go back home with her – to no avail. Nga begged to leave with her sister and Tuyet relented. She then embraced everyone, said goodbye, and tearfully stood aside. She would leave for Phu Loc in the morning.

Hieu and the men had been loading the boat with food and water and now they were tying down the provisions with plastic covers. It was time to leave! He started the motor and it ran smooth and steady. The lines were untied and they ran downriver to the stilt house to pick up the family and the new arrivals. It was two o'clock in the morning when they finally pulled out. They were on schedule. Nga and the children were on board with My Lien and Hieu of course, in spite of not being negotiated, but what could Ong Sau say to that now.

The boat would travel upriver to Chau Doc, then turn southwest and cruise down a canal to Ha Tien on the Gulf. From there they would follow the coast down to Rach Gia Bay and pull up to the landing at the town. Everyone was required to remain quiet on the voyage until they entered the Gulf. Many floating and stilt houses would be passed as well as houseboats and commercial vessels – they were not to be disturbed. People would be awakened and become inquisitive or possibly a threat. Ong Sau was on board and he would make sure that didn't happen!

Rach Gia Bay
April 5, 1988

This was a date that I'll remember forever! We had left Long Xuyen and traveled to Rach Gia town through the remainder of the night and most of the next day. Then we tied up at the rendezvous place after dark.

The remainder of the travelers were already there, patiently waiting while more food and water were loaded on board. I sat at the rear of the boat with Thao and Nga while the new passengers worked their way through the crowd to find seats. There were now fifty-four passengers on board the twenty-four foot boat, sitting side by side, unable to stretch or move around.

The eastern horizon began to turn red behind the adjacent hillside so Ong Sau said to father, "You'll have to leave now before the sun rises and people begin to come around." He then stepped off the boat and waved to everyone, "Good luck, have a good trip!" The engine was started and Ong Sau cast off the lines. It wasn't long before the sun started to rise in the sky as we approached the open sea.

Father soon shut the engine down and raised the sail. He had noticed that a coast guard vessel was bearing down on other boats in the bay so he felt that by sailing slowly along we would appear less obtrusive. It didn't happen, Hieu became anxious and steered straight ahead as the large coast guard power boat headed straight toward us at full speed. As they pulled close by, Hieu lowered the sail and the officer called out, "Where are you going? Your boat looks heavy in the water, what are you carrying in there?"

"We've got a load of Jack fruit to sell. Would you like some?" Hieu replied. And then he added, "We're heading across the bay to sell the rest of our last crop of Jack fruits."

At that moment a speedboat came swiftly by the two craft and made a wake that slightly rocked the coast guard boat then splashed against the side of the heavy set hull of the refugees. "No thanks," the officer shouted, "we're moving on." Slowly the patrol boat pulled away then increased speed as it began pursuit of the fast intruder.

During the course of the patrol boat inquiry, everyone remained quiet and hunkered down. My Lien kept the baby silent while Diem and Thao looked straight ahead to appear innocent. The sea was calm as the fresh gentle breeze filled the sail and slowly moved the boat ahead. Fortunately there were no large waves, the sun was high in the cloudless sky, and the beautiful day was opening a new world for them.

We made it out to sea in the Gulf of Thailand by mid-afternoon. The engine was running smooth through the deep blue waters as the shoreline faded away. The sky was bright with the afternoon sun which reflected off of the now two foot waves like sparkling sequins on a dress. There was no land in sight, father was following the chart with the compass while the silence was broken only by the steady drone of the engine and the conversations of the happy passengers. They were chattering like springtime birds, non-stop.

Soon the relaxed passengers began to become active. People were washing their faces, brushing their teeth, and generally cleaning themselves, much to the concern of father about the liberal use of water. The other children and I began to talk and make friends while adults would occasionally wend their way through the group to the front or rear of the boat to stretch and enjoy the fresh air. Everyone seemed to be enjoying themselves as the faithful boat cut through the small chop of the waves on its way to freedom.

The first few days were pleasurable but the water supply was beginning to run low, beneath the planned daily allotment. Malaysia was still the desired destination and Hieu maintained a steady course which required that their craft run toward the oncoming waves that had now built up into a rolling sea. Some of the people were getting seasick while others lost control and started to vomit. Because of the rise and fall of the small vessel in the trough and crest of the waves, people could not work their way to the rear when sick, so they began to throw up at their seat, next to their side. The steady pounding of the waves eventually caused the planks in the bottom to separate slightly allowing seawater to leak into the hull. A bucket brigade was set up with the men to bail out the boat but seawater had now penetrated the fresh water barrel and contaminated it. So everyone would have to conserve and share what water they had by their sides.

Days slowly turned into night while the hapless crew and passengers struggled to stay afloat and remain calm in spite of the rampant seasickness. Then one night My Lien smelled smoke and called Hieu. "It smells like something is burning," she anxiously cried. Hieu checked the engine and realized that it had overheated and was starting to lock up.

He leaned into the cabin and announced to everyone, "I have bad news, the engine has failed, it overheated and seized up. We can't fix it so we'll have to sail from now on. Let's hope for fair winds." Some of the people looked downcast while others were too weak to respond. Conditions were becoming worse; the sick people that had made room to lie down on the wet floor were developing rashes and the odor from inside the cabin was becoming oppressive due to the inability of the people to clean behind the sick.

I asked mother to let me and Phuc sit outside next to father while he navigated the boat. At first mother was afraid that Phuc might fall overboard but now that he was three years old she felt that I could be careful with him. The strong smell in the confines of the cabin was just overwhelming. We sat inside the bathroom box next to the engine where we could get fresh air and be next to father.

We had a little drinking water, a snack, and a striped scarf to keep the sun off of Phuc. He was a very good boy and remained still all the time while watching the waves and the fish. I made sure that he stayed covered in the hot sun and kept him occupied in the evenings by pointing out the stars that filled the night sky from horizon to horizon. A lot of stories were made up about the stars but a favorite of mine was the fairytale about "Au Co", the beautiful mountain fairy who traveled to heal the sick. One day a monster frightened her and Lac Long Quan, a dragon king from the sea, killed the monster. Au Co married Lac Long and bore an egg that hatched one hundred children. He returned to the sea and Au Co settled in Vietnam where her children became the ancestors of the Vietnamese people. I liked the story because Vietnam women look on her as a heroine and a symbol to fight for their nation and their rights. Phuc loved to hear fairytales and father enjoyed having the children sit next to him while he and the men studied the chart.

Two miserable weeks passed while the vulnerable refugees struggled to survive with the nagging fear of the unknown on their minds. The food and water were gone and the boat was taking on more sea water. Nearly all of the people were sick or weak so My Lien and Nga took turns to scoop out the water. My Lien now became worried for her children. They were outside exposed to the elements with nothing to drink and she started to fear for their lives.

Hieu would occasionally look inside to check the condition of everyone. Some of the people would be resting or asleep. But now others were praying while children were begging for food and water.

I felt so bad for everyone and then one night, Phuc was begging me for water. What could I do? I was desperate, he was becoming dehydrated. My back was hurting from the sunburn and my lips were so dry but I managed to work up some saliva and gave it to him to drink. I didn't complain to mother about the pain, she had enough to worry about.

Nighttime was different. It was cold, so I held Phuc tight against my body and just looked at the stars. They were always beautiful, it helped to keep my mind off of things. It was easy to see lights in the night sky and we could sometimes see lights on the water at a distance but could never make contact.

Once again, another night to have to struggle through, and everyone remained quiet as usual until around midnight when a little girl started to cry. She was begging for water, " Please, please, give me some water, I am so thirsty!" Her pleading continued for three hours until finally it became quiet again. The crying had settled down to small whimpering – then nothing. "She's dead, she's dead!!" her mother screamed. Hieu ran inside and worked his way over to the mother. She had fainted. A relative then wrapped the little girl's body in a blanket.

"What happened? How did she die?" Hieu demanded. The lady holding the girl's body looked up and tearfully said, "She kept crying and begging for water so her mother gave her a sleeping pill, hoping that she'd fall asleep. While the pill was taking affect, the girl continued to ask for water so her mother gave her water out of the wood barrel." Hieu exploded with anger, "You people know that water is contaminated! It has sea water in it – that's what killed her!"

Hieu left the cabin disgusted with the people that were close by the mother – they didn't try to stop her from reaching for water. He looked at his children and a sudden surge of fear overwhelmed him when Phuc began to ask for water. Diem was well aware of the tragedy and continued to gently sing to her little brother as she held him close. Inside the cabin the distraught adults began to pray for the lost child, some to Buddha, some to Quan Am, and still others to Jesus.

They were all still awake during the early hours of the morning when the wind started to build up with huge waves that were as high as the top of the boat. My Lien became frightened and whispered to herself, "This isn't good, we're going to die." She crawled out to the stern of the boat to bring the children inside. The waves were getting larger and the threatening storm made the sky pitch black, there were no longer any stars to be seen. My Lien straightened up to reach for the children but the pounding of the boat into the waves caused her to fall backwards and hit her head on the cabin headboard. She fell with a head wound and Nga helped her back into the cabin where she bandaged the large gash to stop the bleeding.

Hieu quickly tied the box down where Diem and Phuc were sitting while Diem tied herself to the box with the scarf. She held Phuc as tight as she could.

It soon started to thunder with lightning striking everywhere and then the rain began while the waves increased in size causing the boat to ride up on the crest of a wave and then pound down into the trough. The ferocious waves were driving the boat way off course. All Hieu could do was hold the tiller tight to keep the boat from turning broadside to the waves and capsize. Everyone inside was praying for the merciful Thanh Hoang, God of the Village, to save them from drowning. Even Hieu began to despair but he held tight on to the wheel as his thoughts obsessively kept telling him that they were not going to survive.

The passing clouds raced by and began to take strange shapes, white clouds would form over the dark clouds and someone noticed that they were shaped like a dragon or a figure of a God. The shapes faded quickly while the wind increased in strength, howling across the sea and blowing foam off of the whitecapped waves. People inside the boat were tumbling over each other, screaming and crying. The mournful mother held on to her lost child while she mumbled and cried out loud as if she were losing her mind. My Lien held onto Nga and Thao but she was developing a fever.

Their course had changed from southwest to northeast. They had veered off from Malaysia and were heading toward Thailand. The boat was still moving along rapidly through the darkness. Eventually the sea subsided allowing the wind to push the boat faster through the increasingly shallow water. Everyone held on tight when they felt a bump as the hull hit bottom and slid across the sand until the bow landed on the shore. They had stopped!!

For awhile they sat quietly and looked at each other until they realized that they were safe. Slowly the sick, starving, and exhausted survivors crawled out onto the beach and walked toward the woods. Local villagers rushed out to help, they would give everyone shelter and food.

The next morning was bright and sunny when Hieu left his benefactor's house and walked to the beach to inspect the boat. It was now partially covered with sand. A little later some of the boat people came out to help him remove the sand and check the boat. There were a few holes in the hull and some of the boards needed caulking, but it was still seaworthy.

The local inhabitants were sensitive to the needs of their guests. Realizing that weeks without decent food would affect the digestive system, they made hot rice soup and suggested that the refugees eat slowly. These people were very kind and knowledgeable about the needs and comfort of people, from experiences with refugees whom they had encountered before this rescue.

THAILAND

110

BANGKOK FERRY

Courtesy of The CIA World Factbook

My Lien had now recovered to the point where she felt obliged to show her gratitude for the kindness of her hosts. She collected valuables from the other members of her group and added her wedding ring. The gifts were thankfully received since the local people had little to offer but the basic necessities and their good will.

Two weeks passed and our group had regained it's strength. We found out that we were on an island that was part of Thailand. I liked the cream colored sand and the trees near the water's edge. Palm trees and other kinds covered the hills behind the beach with green mountains in the distance. But I don't remember the name of that island, there were so many along the coast of Thailand – all beginning with Ko, like Ko Lan or Ko Samet.

Our boat had been repaired and now the islanders politely asked us to leave. They said that the government would not allow any more refugees. So father supervised the loading of the boat and was careful to place the drinking water in a protected container.

To my surprise, twenty-four more aliens joined our party in the afternoon and boarded the boat. We didn't have any choice, they had to leave too! This small craft was now going to have to carry seventy-eight passengers. Father was concerned but what could he do, we had to leave the island that very afternoon!!

———————————————

———————————————

BOATS AT SEA

CHAPTER 7

MALAYSIA

"Pirates and Friends"

They didn't waste any time! The local people tied a line to our boat and started to pull us out to sea with their motorized fishing boat. This time our cabin was so crowded with people that no one would be able to lie down if they got sick.

My father tried to work on the engine once more as we moved along. Other men made suggestions but to no avail – it would not start. We finally reached international waters and the villagers cast off our bow line while father raised the sail. It billowed out and we started to make headway.

Some of the passengers began to grumble when the wind died down. They expressed a desire to go back to the island and even began to paddle once they got the boat turned around. An appeal would be made to the government to accept them as legal immigrants. The situation had gotten completely out of control!

A little while later one of the passengers shouted that he had seen a large Thailand Navy vessel heading out to sea and now it had changed course and was bearing down on us. The disgruntled passengers continued to paddle toward the coast though until a large splash on the water in front of us was followed by a loud boom. It was a cannon! Sailors could be seen reloading the 3in/50 caliber cannon while two other sailors pointed and aimed the weapon. Another round was fired that landed closer to us on the right side. Spray from the splash washed over our boat followed by another boom. They had our range!

Everyone panicked and paddled the boat around until it headed back out to sea. The patrol boat then turned away and began to move up the coast. We could see the many sailors with all kinds of guns on the large vessel which was at least one hundred and fifty feet long. It slid smoothly through the water as it picked up speed and faded into the distance.

There was only one thing to do – head toward Malaysia as we had planned. The sail soon picked up the wind and we were comfortable with the fact that we had plenty of food and water to sustain us for a long time. Father must have been enraged with these people that mutinied against him considering everything he had done for them.

It was smooth sailing for three days until another large boat approached us. Father and the other men were hopeful that the boat might consider a tow or offer to help us in some way. But as they closed almost within shouting distance, father told all of the women and children to stay inside while all of the men were to be visible out in the open. I was hiding in the small box with Phuc. I covered him with the striped scarf as the dark hulled larger boat slowly approached us and bumped alongside. They tossed grappling lines to secure our boat and kept their engine running at idling speed.

I peeked through a little hole in the box and saw a sight that frightened me. It looked like something from the gates of hell. There were men stationed around their boat with long knives. The sarongs wrapped around their waists indicated that they were from Thailand. Their skin was dark with numerous tattoos on their arms and necks. Some were bare from the waist up with shaved heads or short pony tails. Their fierce countenance soon betrayed their intentions – PIRATES!!!

Hieu quickly informed the men of the menace facing them. He told the men to all step outside and block the view of the women inside. "Don't let these people catch a glimpse of our women!" he pleaded. One of the raiders put his leg across the side and stepped into the refugee boat. He straddled both boats and began to talk in Thai language but no one understood. He then expressed his demands in sign language for valuables and jewelry to be collected and passed over to him. To make his point clear, two of the crew stepped into the captive boat and began to hit the men with the flat of their knives and the handles. Hieu quickly grabbed the long wooden oar and confronted the two pirates – they stopped in their tracks.

This standoff angered the spokesman and he began to shout for the possessions of the passengers. He offered to leave if they would comply with his wishes. Hieu struggled to comprehend the demand and realized that if he could give them enough, they would leave without causing harm. He entered the cabin and collected rings, bracelets, wedding bands, and other jewelry and returned to the deck.

That wasn't enough! They wanted to look inside. All of the husbands and male family members then stood up and banded together in front of the outnumbered thieves. Hieu reached out with the collected items, the leader looked the passengers over, took the booty, then recalled his men. They then withdrew their lines and pulled away. Everyone on the victimized craft stood motionless until the menacing boat was just a small stern in the distance.

I also watched them leave. My heart was pounding so fast, I thought that I would faint. Little Phuc had been terrific, I released him and thanked him for being so quiet. We were very lucky because a good many of the people on board had members of their families raped and killed while on their own boats. Their boats had been taken, leaving them stranded on the island where they joined us. Some even had to swim ashore while others drowned. Yes, we were very lucky, and I have to thank my father for that – he was a brave man and my hero!!

Hieu now had total command and respect. He studied the map, observed the wind and determined what direction to take – we were going to Malaysia! Everyone was confident now. We had a good following wind and a strong leader. After a few days of pleasant sailing, an island was seen in the distance. We had no idea which island it was but father headed straight for it. I think he knew where he was going because after some of the men jumped overboard to push us ashore, a crowd of people stood on the nearby dock waving a large sign – "Welcome – Pulau Bidong Refugee Camp."

PULAU BIDONG

We all cheered and cried. The rest of the men then jumped overboard and pushed the boat to the dock while a large Vietnamese group stood by to catch the lines and tie us to the landing. Some of the people on shore gave the appearance that they were looking for family members, relatives, or friends.

Hieu waited until everyone got safely off the boat – with the help of their new-found friends. The elders especially needed their assistance. All the while My Lien was crying with happiness, they had almost made it to the promised land! Hieu made one more check through the boat to see if any of the belongings or personal items had been left behind. He then rounded up his family and gear and headed toward the administration building.

I remember seeing all of the people along the way. Some were directing us to the center while others just looked to see if we resembled someone. Still others shouted questions about where we were from or who we were related to – it was almost overwhelming – we felt like celebrities. These people had the same dreams that we did – to find a home and freedom!

Pulau Bidong was an uninhabited island off of Kualu Terengganu, Malaysia. It served as a protected refugee staging area by the Malaysian government and was overseen by the International Red Cross. From there the people would be sent to the United States, Canada, Australia, or several of the European countries. At times the halfway houses were at a premium because the capacity for 4500 refugees would be overrun by 20,000 people. It took time to receive approval for applicants to be accepted in one of the foster countries. Those unfortunate enough to be rejected were sent to Sungai Besi Camp to be repatriated to Vietnam after the war. This had to be a frightening hardship for those families that had connections to the South Vietnam regimes or were affluent enough to be considered supportive of the former government.

Initially, the local wildlife was decimated by the need for food but once the Red Cross was established, supplies were shipped on a regular basis. Long-houses and offices were built from the local wood with electricity and water supplied to facilitate schools and workplaces as well as the homes.

Eventually the camp grew to become a civilized community – post office, tailors, hair salons, even a church and temple. Part of the beach was named China Beach, Pantai Cina, after a famous beach in Vietnam. The area had become a mini-Saigon!

Hieu was excited upon seeing the surrounding buildings and busy people. He quickly walked to the administration center where he was greeted by the friendly officials. We soon arrived and were given clothing and other necessities while our housing and food allotments were being assigned.

MALAYSIA

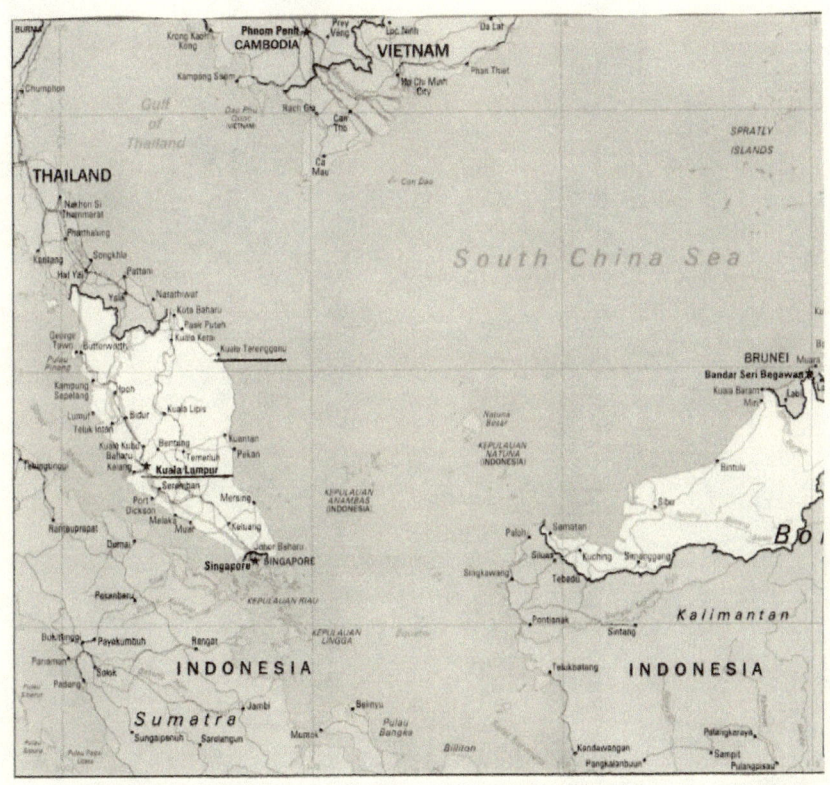

Courtesy of the University of Texas Libraries, The University of Texas at Austin

PETRONAS TOWERS IN KUALA LUMPUR

Courtesy of The CIA World Factbook

With Malaysia having been a former British colony, the people developed a colloquial or street English language known as Manglish. In later years, a more formal English emerged as Malaysian English and it is now taught in the schools and spoken as a second language. Even though the official Malaysian language is Bahasa Malaysia or Malay, English was being used on Pulau Bidong so that Vietnamese translators could communicate between the government and the refugees.

Our translator's name was Khai and he was assigned to take us to our quarters. The island is divided into four quadrants – north, south, east, and west with newcomers assigned to the western quadrant. We reached the two story building that was constructed of wood and corrugated tin and climbed the stairs. It was a typical island building – a very plain and basic structure with a flat roof. There were twenty sections, one for each family. We were assigned to the fourth section from the stairs. Our section was a three walled windowless room with a fourth outside wall consisting of a long curtain that could be raised or lowered.

The Malaysian government provided weekly allotments of food. Each family received one chicken, five bunches of vegetables, and seven packs of instant noodles for every member. Any other groceries or drinks beyond water had to be purchased from small vendors on the island. The fortunate refugees who received money from relatives in the host countries were able to operate the small stores that carried the much sought after herbs, fish and soy sauces, and other scarce commodities. The only constraint was the Malaysian government restriction on pork and other meats that violated their religious practices.

We were anxious to get settled and it didn't take long. Within two days our surroundings had become familiar, in fact, father had already made new friends. He had volunteered to join the neighborhood patrol with other Vietnamese who had been associated with the United States military. Their function was to provide security for the camp to prevent any theft or physical harm to the refugees.

This was a tall order, there were thousands of transients waiting to be relocated, some with contacts or family in the United States and elsewhere, while others were searching for sponsors. Everyone had to be processed and transferred to the main distribution center at Sungai Besi which could take months or even years. So the best thing to do was to settle down and make the best of this temporary home.

A short time later, Khai, the translator, came to our humble abode to have a meeting with father and the family. We were told that there would be an interview with the Malaysian government at the administration building. An application would then be forwarded to the United Nations High Commission for Refugees (UNHCR).

Everyone was nervous, we all had to be interviewed separately, I guess to corroborate our story. We had to prove that we were political refugees as defined by the United Nations or at least had a close relative in another country to sponsor us. After hearing that almost eighty percent of the applicants were rejected in later years after the war because most emigrants at that time were considered to be economic migrants, we thought that we would be sent back to Vietnam.

It was strictly business!

"Why do you want to leave Vietnam?"

"Do you have a family member in another country?"

"Do you have any relatives that are also refugees here or at another location?"

Hieu certainly had all the answers. He had served in the South Vietnam Army and had been imprisoned by the Communists for six years. He also had a sister-in-law, Thu Hoa, at Sungai Besi with her children. His situation was unquestionably political! That settled it, we were accepted!! It was like a weight had been lifted from our shoulders and Hieu was told that they would try to locate his older sister who was living in the United States. We would now have to wait but we could taste freedom!

A few nights went by while we tried to restore some sense of normalcy. But we kept losing our food and could not figure out what was happening to it. One night while Hieu was making his rounds on the patrol he passed our place and suddenly heard a loud noise. At first he thought it was an intruder but when he turned his flashlight on to our ceiling, there was a string of rats suspended from the ceiling down to our food. They held each other by the tail to make the chain.

My Lien jumped up and screamed. Hieu shined his light on the outside of the building and saw rats as numerous as ants on a hill. Needless to say, we didn't sleep that night. My Lien laid in bed all night with her eyes open while Hieu thought about ways to protect the food in the future. It would be a continuous battle.

On the other hand, evenings were enjoyable on occasion when the government agents played a movie against the outside wall of the administration center. They set up a projector while everyone gathered around without chairs. Some enterprising people carved the hillside into a staircase so that everyone could sit down.

The films were mostly educational documentaries about the United States – the types of cultures, religions, and holidays. They were quite entertaining to us since we would have to become acclimated to our new home.

There was a humorous incident one evening when we couldn't get a seat to watch the movie. My brother Thao said that he had a plan. He had captured two rats and tied strings to their tails. When he returned to the arena with his captives, he released them on the strings and they ran through the seating area. People panicked and ran in all directions - we had our choice of seats!

Our family did make the best of our situation. Everyone was upbeat and positive and the mischievous ways of the children confirmed that fact. We had become footloose and carefree to the point that only a sense of security could provide.

Hieu and My Lien also enjoyed the temporary surroundings and Hieu with his inquisitive nature had been exploring the island. It was a beautiful day when Hieu came running toward the house to get My Lien to come and see the special place that he had found. Together they ran toward a hill and passed a grove of wild berry bushes, then numerous bee hives – bees everywhere. Hidden behind the berry bushes was a cave overlooking the ocean. The view was spectacular! Later they gathered the children and returned to the cave. It would become the children's secret hideout and they would spend a lot of time there.

A month later, while playing in the area, Thao and I heard a loud scream coming from the bottom of the cave. We ran home and brought father back to investigate. He found out that some men had been fishing and had caught several hammer-head sharks and a baby shark. Somehow, a couple of the men had been bitten by the sharks, either by standing in the water while fishing or after landing the sharks. They were bleeding heavily and one man's leg was gone. I looked down into the water from up above and saw many sharks swimming around in the cave's lagoon. We found out that sharks were everywhere around the island and that was bad for fishing.

After a while we decided to go home, it was getting late and the sky had darkened with a threatening storm approaching our side of the island. The wind soon changed from the prevailing direction and the driven rain started to pound down on to the dirt roads creating mud that nearly stopped all traffic. This weather front lasted for days and prevented the cargo ship from delivering our food supply.

What stock we had was soon depleted. People tried to go fishing in the shark infested waters but they couldn't catch quantities enough to feed everyone. We had no recourse – we had to hunt rats! Fires were made so that we could blow smoke through the rat holes. We caught about ten of them when they scurried out for air. They were skinned and cooked over a charcoal fire. We couldn't complain under the circumstances, they tasted rather like chicken!

It is amazing how resilient children can be when surrounded by a loving family. Perhaps we took advantage of the situation for we became quite naughty. One afternoon while most folks were taking their usual nap, we decided to have some fun. We located several people that were asleep in their hammocks and tied toilet paper to their toes. We lit the paper and ran away to watch. They all jumped up and stamped their feet up and down while shouting some very angry and sometimes coarse words – to put it politely! It was great fun, we would snicker and imitate the fire dance but we only played that game for a couple of times to avoid being caught.

There were many things for the children to do during these times. We would watch the adults play Chinese checkers or cards from a deck that was made out of cigarette packages. Every time there was a full moon, we went to the beach to catch fish and dig for clams. When the tide was extra low we would pull up rocks and find neat little creatures such as sea urchins and crabs – it was our favorite thing to do on the island.

The most exciting adventure to be had was to visit the partially sunken navy ships that were destroyed during World War Two. Parts of the ships were above water and embedded in the sand. The Japanese had invaded the north side of western Malaysia in 1941 and fought their way down to Singapore by February of 1942. On the way, they captured thousands of overwhelmed British and Australian troops, most of whom died on death marches similar to Bataan.

On Pulau Redang, the largest island in the group of islands off of the Malaysian coast that included Pulau Bidong, there are two historic shipwrecks, the HMS Prince of Wales and the HMS Repulse. These bombing casualties opened the way for Japanese occupation.

I remember the large warships on our island with cannon still menacingly pointed toward the sky. One day my brother dared me to go inside one of them – I was afraid but I went anyway! I climbed up the gangway and stepped onto the deck. The hull and bulkheads were covered with rust and seashells. As I carefully made my way into the dark recesses of the interior, I let out a shout to reassure myself. A loud echo then reverberated along the walls and frightened me. I reacted and drew in a deep breath of the foul smelling sea air.

I quickly felt my way along to get outside of this ghost ship and grabbed a piece of loose board on the way. An impulsive bang with the board against the wall created another loud echo and knocked some of the rust loose with small pieces falling on my head and shoulders. My hasty exit made my brother laugh so hard – it wasn't fair, I almost wet my pants!

In spite of being teased by my brother, we still ventured over to the cave every day. We loved to pick the wild red berries with their sweet smell and taste. And one day we saw watermelon growing along side the hill. I wondered how that happened as I stooped to pick one of the ripe ones. Suddenly my brother hit me along- side the head and said not to eat those melons. People must have been eating them there and passing the seeds that they swallowed. That's how they came to grow there – how gross!

Oh well, we kept going to our cave until other people discovered it and took over our hideaway. We were very happy during those times, my parents were together at last and it made us all feel good to see how happy and loving they were with each other.

Three months had quickly passed by when one day Khai stopped by to give us good news. They had located my aunt in the United States, dad's older sister Kym. And they had also located mother's sister as well. It had been confirmed that Thu Hoa and her children were at the main refugee camp – Sungai Besi, Malaysia.

My Lien cried with happiness when she learned that Hieu and she and the children were going to be transferred to Sungai Besi – there would be a reunion! Not realizing that she was pregnant with her fourth child, My Lien and Hieu gathered all of their belongings to be ready for their departure the next day. That evening they all went out to enjoy the beautiful sunset from the hillside. They had heard that boats would be arriving that evening and the next day so they wanted to be part of the welcoming crowd.

Early the next morning as we were heading toward the pier to embark on the cargo ship, another boat slowly pulled up loaded with people. There was a frightened look on their faces as if they had encountered a terrible experience. We overheard some of the conversations. They had been robbed by pirates and their boat was ransacked. Men were clubbed and knifed, then thrown into the sea. Young women were raped while the other pirates clapped and cheered. Their parents were forced to watch the brutality until some of the victims hemorrhaged and bled to death. Other stories cannot be repeated, they were too gruesome to even recall.

As we started to walk away, we heard that these pitiful people were left on the ocean to starve. They resorted to cannibalism. I looked over and saw a woman come ashore with a handbag. It had an arm sticking out of it. My Lien said a prayer as we passed.

I remember later how I responded when someone mentioned to me that the boat people were just homeless. "No," I replied, "the boat people have a home, it's at the bottom of the sea. Tens of thousands ended up there."

We boarded the large, steel cargo boat, it was like a tramp steamer. Soon we were fed soup and bread while the boat was underway. It made good time, we arrived at the port of entry, Kuantan, in three hours. From there our group boarded buses to carry us to Sungai Besi. It was a long trip, about a day and a half. Sometimes we could go 100 kilometers in an hour yet other times in rural areas it could take a whole day to go 10 kilometers.

SUNGAI BESI

1988

The road from Kuantan to Kuala Lumpur where Sungai Besi was located, ran halfway across country until it reached the town of Temerloh. From there the Titiwangsa Mountain Range had to be crossed. It ran from Thailand southeast almost to Singapore. We went around mountains and through tunnels, a lot of tunnels. Our layover at night was at a rest stop's vacant building where we ate our noodles and slept on the floor with blankets provided by the proprietors. Inland Malaysia is hot and humid most of the year so mosquitoes swarmed all night. It was a relief to be back on the bus for an early departure.

When we reached the bus station at our destination, there was the usual crowd waiting to see if any familiar faces could be found. I noticed a boy standing there scratching his head, he looked like my cousin Nam, Aunt Thu Hoa's second son. I yelled out to mother to look, he was jumping up and down, he was so happy. He called out my name and shouted to all of my family. He then turned and called out to his mother – Thu Hoa came running and slowly worked her way through the crowd. We had a grand reunion! She cried all the way to the administration building while holding on to me.

The Malaysian government official showed us our quarters and provided food until we could get on the distribution list. When we reached our bungalow, a one floor ranch type house with a curtain for a front door, everyone started to talk and share news. All of my cousins were there, Nam, Hai, and Dui. They were excited to see me and my brothers and they told us all about the fun places to visit. It seemed like the living conditions would be about the same as Pulau Bidong.

We were all so happy! I wasn't even listening to what they were telling me. My father joined the night watch patrol that evening and quickly made friends. Mother was already thinking about ways to make money because the government only supplied the bare food essentials again like Pulau Bidong. It just wasn't enough for all of us so My Lien would make the rounds in the neighborhood offering her tailoring services. She was quite good at fixing shirt sleeves, sewing on buttons, altering clothes, and mending holes. In addition, she would bake cakes for sale at the market along with the much requested French bread. It reminded me of the times back home when I would be half asleep in the early morning as Grandmother began to bake cake. The steamy smell of the coconut and vanilla mung beans would fill the springtime air that flowed gently across the rice fields. Even the neighbors would be awakened along with me to the sweet promise of an early treat.

At this time the camp population was about 5,000 people, somewhat lower than the number of people a few years ago. There were fences around the perimeter but food vendors could obtain access to sell their wares, so if some folks could obtain money from their United States relatives, they could exchange it for Malaysian money and purchase food.

The Malaysian dollar was called a "Ringit" and it was divided into 100 sens with varying coin sizes from 5, 10, 20, to 50 sens. The exchange rate was about 2.5 ringits to one American dollar. An advantage for folks receiving money from United States relatives. Ironically in 1988, the year we were there, the country suffered from the Malaysian Constitution Crisis. The heads of state were disputing the power of the three branches of government. The supreme court had formerly exercised independent judicial power to the point of pilfering public funds for personal expenses and luxuries. The newly elected prime minister said that the legislative and executive branches must oversee the power of the court. He then sacked three judges and had constitutional amendments passed giving the courts judicial power as Parliament might grant them. There was concern in the camps that the status of the refugees might be affected if civil unrest erupted. Fortunately, the government remained stable and secure.

There were rules and they were enforced. The camp closed at 9 pm and reopened at 9 am. If you were late on arrival at night, admittance was refused. My father started his night watch with the crew at precisely 9pm. He would patrol the grounds with his flashlight and he took his job very seriously. We could forget about eating pork – it was forbidden by the Malaysian religion.

Food pickup at the administration center was once a week. The camp was divided into four sections for distribution, A, B, C, and D. We would report with B group to get the unchanging but consistent supply of chicken, vegetables, instant noodles, and fruits occasionally. Drinking water was also supplied to prevent any outbreak of disease from tainted water that could be obtained from rain barrels or springs.

We were always glad to have Aunt Nga come along, this would guarantee extra food – especially since the food handler liked her. But mother was very strict in that regard, dating was forbidden. Unfortunately, there would sometimes be arguments among the refugees about the food and water that they received. There must have been some disparity about the portions given out. Fighting would even break out and the guards and attendants would have to be called. The hollow eyed children would peer through the fences at the outbreak with frightened eyes at the violence engulfing their families. It was sad but I still looked forward to those days because mother would always make "Canh ga" that evening, one of my favorite meals – chicken soup!

In support of the rigid discipline that was imposed on the camp, Malaysian officials demanded inspections of the bungalows. They would search throughout the house for illicit drugs and food – namely pork. Since there was a substantial Chinese population in the country that did eat pork, a continuous effort was taken to be sure pork did not enter the campground. To no avail, Chinese people knew that the refugees wanted pork, so at night they would throw a rock over the fences to get attention or make some sort of signal. It was a risky endeavor to evade the guards, including my father who may or may not have turned a blind eye to this unlawful activity. But we did get our pork!

Then one day a letter arrived from my father's sister Kym. She sent us one hundred dollars from California. Dad went to the money exchange and purchased clothes for us and extra food for mother since she was now pregnant. Of course the money didn't last too long so my mother continued to save the instant noodles to trade for food that we children would enjoy. One day she had enough noodles to trade for three apples. Oh the sweet fresh smell of that apple! My mouth used to water when I just passed the fruit vendor and now we had some to eat. My mother brought the apples home then washed and peeled them. We all shared the apples except mother who ate the skins. I felt sad for her who always seemed to sacrifice for us, it made me love her that much more.

Two more months went by and a great announcement was made – Thu Hoa and her children were leaving for the camp in the Philippines. They had located her husband in California. We all were very sad about the departure but that was our goal.

Mother's pregnancy required more paperwork and processing for clearance so we continued to abide our time. It wasn't long after that when she gave birth to Duyen, a little sister for me. Duyen was tiny, she only weighed five pounds but she had a beautiful dark complexion. When mother came home from the hospital I got the chance to hold my only sister for the first time. When her little eyes looked at me I selfishly felt like she was all mine. I even made a deal with Thao, if mom has a boy, Thao would take care of him. But now I will take care of Duyen.

My Lien couldn't breast feed because of the medication she needed. So Diem would bottle feed the baby and sing to her while rocking her to sleep. They had strung a hammock between the walls and Diem would lie there with her new friend.

During the mornings we had to attend classes to learn about American culture and the language. In the afternoons, I ran straight home to take care of Duyen. When I arrived, she would always hold up her arms and cry for me. How nice to have her miss me!

Five more months had passed by when we got a call to report to the administration for a final interview. It had been almost twelve months since we left Rach Gia Bay and fourteen months since we started to plan the trip. Both of my parents were very nervous in spite of the preliminary approval that they had received. While they were waiting, they saw people leaving the building in tears for having been rejected. They would have to stay in camp or return to Vietnam.

We all walked stiffly into the office, dressed in our finest clothes, and sat quietly down. The Malaysian officer would speak and our translator would interpret. He quickly said -

"Your file was approved."

Oh my, we will leave camp next week for the Philippines. My parents were overjoyed. Dad had a party that night and invited his night watch friends. I'm not sure but they may have had some "bia". Dad liked his beer. Then I began to think – What does America look like? Are people really white with yellow hair? And all those houses and cars! It's too much for me to think about!

CHAPTER 8

LOS ANGELES

"Home of The Brave"

It was time to leave. We packed our clothing and a few personal items and said goodbye with mixed emotions to our bungalow – there had been some happy times there. Mother packed all the noodles that she had saved to use as bargaining money.

The trip would be long. We had to leave from Kuala Lumpur, the capital and largest city in Malaysia, soon to be home of the famous Petronas Twin Towers, and travel cross country again to the east coast to catch a ship. From there we would head northeast across the South China Sea and pass the Spratly Islands to reach Luzon, the northernmost island of the Philippines. There were two camps located a little south of Manila on Luzon – Palawan and Bataan. We would be heading for the Philippine Refugee Processing Center (PRPC) near Morong, Bataan.

All refugees arriving there had received confirmation that they had been accepted for resettlement in the west. So the general atmosphere among the population was positive and upbeat. The purpose of the camp was to help Vietnamese, Cambodian, and Laotian refugees plus ethnic minorities from these countries to adapt to their new surroundings.

There would be health checks, especially for tuberculosis, completion of

135

documentation, and an opportunity to learn English as a second language (ESL). This program was funded by the United States Department of State and operated by the International Catholic Migration Commission (ICMC). It provided training to adults aged 17 to fifty-five. In addition, Cultural Orientation (CO) and Work Orientation (WO) was offered. Children would be taught a similar ESL program by the World Relief Organization. This would be an extensive classroom primary education program.

PHILIPPINES

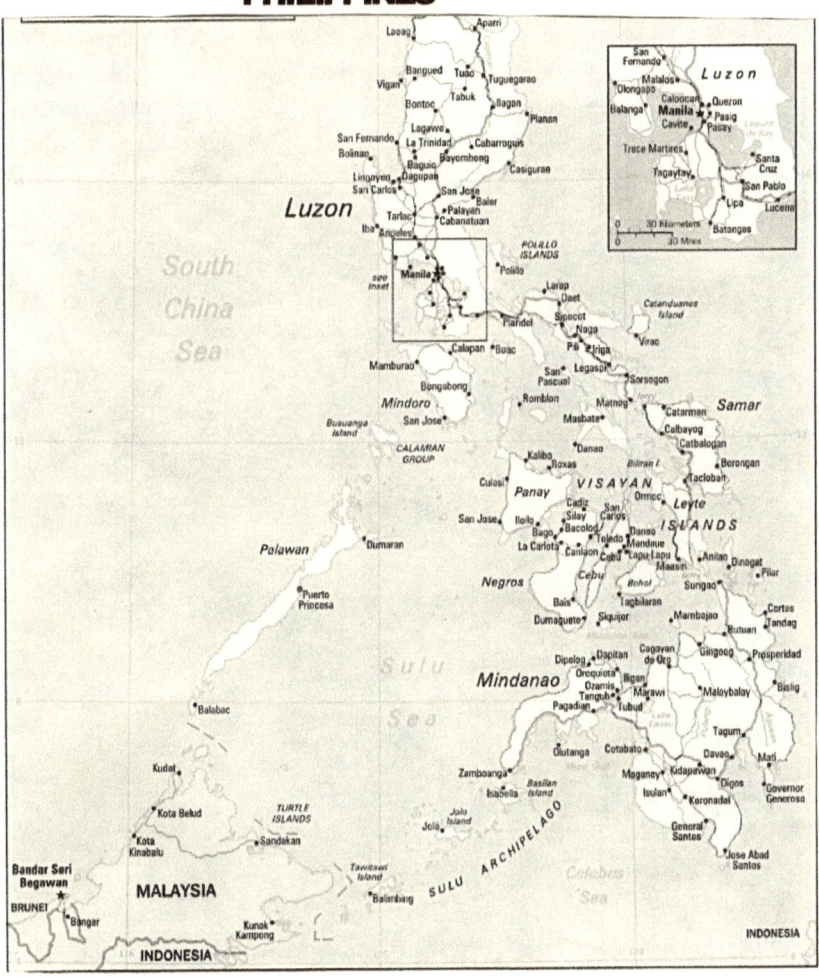

Courtesy of the University of Texas Libraries, The University of Texas at Austin

SPANISH LIGHTHOUSE ON CORREGIDOR

Courtesy of The CIA World Factbook

We arrived at four o'clock in the afternoon. Surprisingly, there were no fences, everything was open for residents to come and go and for outside vendors and neighbors to visit. Another town had been developed for the refugees, only better, and it was divided into four sections. Section one was located on a hill, section two was near the market and fortunately that was our assignment. We would be sheltered in one of the ten houses on the main street. Section three was near the school and section four was close to the administration center.

Mother and father were very excited to be here – there were no restrictions on movement and everyone knew that they had the promise of a bright future. The administrative people were very courteous, once we got settled they came by the house to escort us around the town and to show us the rules and time constraints. Everyone had to attend school with the emphasis that it was for their own benefit.

It was fun being back in school again, Phu Loc seemed like a long time ago. I remember my teacher, Ms. Joyce, she was very tall and somewhat portly, and she had the nicest smile that complimented her freckled face. She must have liked me a lot because she always offered me snacks after school – maybe she felt sorry for me because I was the smallest girl in the class. Once in a while she would have me and other students over to her house for lunch, that was very kind of her. And school was interesting and fun; we learned more about American culture, history and holidays, and their religions. But most importantly, we learned English. There had been some exposure to American life before at the movies at Pulau Bidong and the classes at Sungai Besi, but these classes were more extensive and disciplined.

Of course there must always be an occasional setback or crisis – things can't always be smooth else you wouldn't appreciate the good times when you had them. Phuc got lost one day and we were all in a panic, especially mother. He was a cute little boy who always kept himself neat and clean, dirty feet or shirts were not tolerated.

Our concern was the possibility of a kidnapping. Hours went by slowly as we searched everywhere. Finally we had to file a missing persons report. Everyone was distraught and miserable. We sat outside of the house and were soon mercifully distracted by a group of cows that were being driven

BATAAN, LUZON

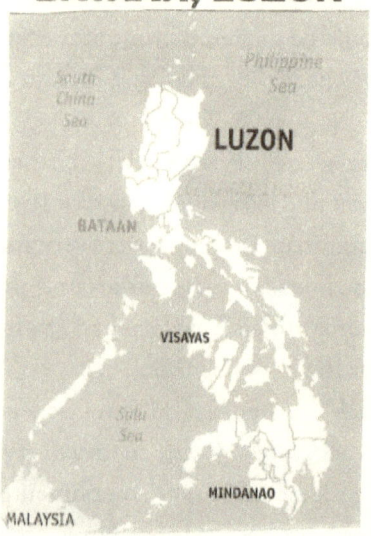

Courtesy of UC Irvine Libraries by Project Ngoc, Photographer

through the streets. But the odor was overwhelming from the manure and everyone moved away. Then someone shouted that little Phuc was seen walking behind the cattle. He was crying as he moved along because he couldn't avoid stepping into the mess – but more likely because he dreaded the confrontation that was awaiting him. When asked about his whereabouts, he said that he had gone to a movie down the street to watch Bruce Lee and Jackie Chan. Well that did it – he got a good spanking and well deserved! Later he confided to me that it was worth it, he loved to watch the action movies!

Shopping was now very accessible. The Philippine citizens were allowed to sell or trade merchandise from their stores to the refugees. One family even bought a large screen television and set up a mini-movie theatre. Not all of the refugees were poor, some had even brought along gold bullion. There were even goldsmiths in residence making jewelry. The affluent family with the theatre made more money by charging people to watch their films, mostly Chinese martial art. And many attended the shows when not in school.

We settled in to our surroundings rather quickly. Food was delivered once a week, mother was offering her tailoring services as usual along with the cakes and bread for the nearby market, and we all learned a lot about basic English and the United States. There was one inconvenience though, the largest bathroom that I had ever seen had been built for the colony. We would have to carry a bucket of water along to flush the toilets. But that wasn't bad and with all of the activity and distractions, time slipped by before we knew it.

In fact, seven months had passed by when we received notice that we would be leaving for California. We finally made it, our journey had taken us twenty-one months to reach our goal but we did it. I felt like I was going to heaven because the programs on television had shown that everyone had refrigerators, dishwashers, large televisions, electric stoves, in-door plumbing, and lights. This was completely different from our clay stove that used wood to cook and charcoal to bake, no electric appliances there! They even used metal silverware, not chopsticks or bamboo spoons that we had to make. Back in Phu Loc we either walked or rode a bike. And the cars, it was unbelievable – so many and so beautiful! I couldn't wait to see what

America looked like, did people really have yellow hair and snow white skin? The night before our departure I just couldn't sleep, too many thoughts and questions had raced through my mind.

Well, this was our final day. There was a total of twenty-five families leaving our camp. Nine families were going to the United States and the rest were departing for Canada and Australia. Only five of the families were going to California. My father's sister Kym had told us to leave everything because she would have new clothes and necessities for us upon our arrival. So my parents gave everything away to our neighbors, all we had left were the clothes on our back and the necessary documents for travel.

Oh, the plane was so large! Three seats in the middle with two extra seats on the window sides. I sat next to Thao and Phuc while mother, dad, little sister Duyen, and Aunt Nga, sat together. We were given food but I was too excited to eat, it tasted different anyway. I couldn't wait to see the new world – was everything there really true?

September 9, 1989

As we made our approach to the airport, I could see land extending out into the blue Pacific water. It was a peninsula, Palos Verdes Peninsula, I later learned. America at last!! To the left of the peninsula was the Los Angeles airport. We slowly descended and I stretched to look out of the port side window and saw Marina Del Ray with all the beautiful boats.

The plane taxied up to the terminal and we walked through the gate to pass through the customs inspection station. The first thing I saw was a six foot giant of a black woman, hair braided with different colors and nails so long that they curled together. She was wearing a poncho and I was so scared that I held on tight to my mother's legs. I was shaking like some wet dog!

But the frightening lady held up a sign that said, "Tang Hieu family." She was actually there to greet us. My father walked toward her and said that he was Hieu Tang. She then held up her hand for us to wait while she made a phone call for a translator to come down and meet us. It was obvious we didn't speak English well in spite of the lessons. We were soon told by the translator that father's sister was not able to pick us up, so a social worker

142

would take us to her house. Three more hours were then spent at the airport to get through customs and then the seven of us departed in a minivan.

Everything was different! The roads were so smooth and the houses looked nice and large – all made with brick. I couldn't keep up with all the cars passing by as we drove up the 405 freeway. Even the trees were different. I soon fell asleep though.

I was awakened when our social worker lady called out that we had arrived at my aunt's apartment. She led the way and knocked on the door. The young person that answered was Kym's daughter Keely. She spoke English fluently and signed the release statement for us although she didn't seem too happy about it. We entered the two bedroom apartment and Keely called for her mother. Kym appeared and I noticed that she looked a lot like my father as he gave her a hug.

For some reason she ignored the rest of us. I could tell that mother seemed to be worried, it was obvious that there would not be enough room for all of us. Then she spoke up and asked Kym if we could get settled and look at the clothes and toiletries that had been purchased. We were all shocked when Kym insolently said that nothing was bought, we would have to purchase the clothing ourselves.

Mother was devastated but she remained civil when she reminded Kym that we were told to leave our things behind. Abruptly she added that we would have to find a store right away. "There's a Goodwill store down the road," Kym replied. "Can you take us there?" mother asked.

"No, I don't have time for that," she answered with a disrespectful tone.

My parents went outside and started to talk to the maintenance man. He graciously volunteered to escort us to the store. I was excited about looking through all those aisles for clothes. And since school would be starting soon, mother bought us each five sets of clothing with the money she had earned at Bataan. While walking the five miles back to the apartment, she started to cry but composed herself after awhile and said, "We'll be all right, just do the best we can, be strong, do the right thing and we'll be all right." Then she wiped away more tears. After all she'd been through, she must have suffered from emotional exhaustion. I felt so sad for her that I reacted and made a promise to myself that I would be really good and helpful. Looking back on this frustrating time when our expectations had been so high, I think we must have been faithfully adhering to an ancient Buddha quote – "Those who are free of resentful thoughts surely find peace."

The moment of truth had arrived. It was the first day of school at Eisenhower Elementary and I would be in the sixth grade. I got my assigned class from the principal's office and entered the room. Mrs. Fishbach stood there like a Native American Princess. She wore a long white skirt to accent her height and beautiful long white hair. Over that was a white sweater with large puffy shoulders. A large brown belt and sandals provided the finishing touches to a stunning display of fashionable splendor.

She immediately clapped her hands to get the attention of the children and then in a soft velvet voice she welcomed me. I felt very comfortable right away and before the day was out I had met a Vietnamese girl called Hien whom I could talk to in our native language. Being a newcomer herself, we had a lot of things in common. The class itself was a melting pot of ethnic minorities. Out of the twenty-eight students, fourteen were Caucasian, five were Vietnamese, and the remaining nine were Hispanic.

I tried to fit in with my jean skirt, green sweater, and a nice pair of Keds tennis shoes. Mrs. Fishbach took an interest in my desire to learn more English, she encouraged me to talk a lot with her and she gave me a book to take home and read along with some stick-on high lighters to mark certain words. Hien and I also became good friends, so I was happy to be in this nice school.

Dad would always be waiting for me outside of school at three-thirty. He liked to walk me home and talk about my day. But one day there was a sadness about him, I could see it in his eyes. I was too shy to inquire so we quietly walked home. As I entered the door, the food smelled delicious, mother had made Pho but Aunt Kym was very angry. She shouted to mother that she couldn't stand the smell – the odor filled the whole apartment. So we all ate outside on the patio – the house was just too crowded and mother was feeling sad again. Keely had to leave her bedroom and move in with her mother. My mother, father, Aunt Nga, and Duyen had to sleep with me in one bed while Thao and Phuc slept in the kitchen.

And every woman needs her own kitchen, the old adage that two hands spoil the pot was true.

To add insult to injury, Kym's husband, another Nam, came back after being apart from her for ten years. She refused to sleep with him even though they had been legally married in Vietnam – he stayed in the living room. The place was worse than a boarding house!

Of course, in addition to the housing problem, the children still had their little episodes. One day Thao couldn't find his lunch card, he was afraid to tell mother, so he went to school anyway. As usual, dad would also walk us to school even though it was only 6 am when we left the house. We would swing by the junior high that Thao attended then continue on to the elementary school.

What I liked most about the school was the lunch menu. I could have orange juice or a grilled cheese sandwich and I could also eat breakfast there. But today I wondered what Thao was going to do without his lunch card. My father knew that he was going to be hungry so he brought along a snack when he came to pick us up. Thao gulped the food down and said with his mouth full that we needed to get home right away so that he could find the card.

Mother had dinner ready when we arrived, another favorite Vietnam dish of cooked rice and "canh chua ca" – sweet and sour soup. Kym continued to refuse to eat with us and now she was insisting that her husband and daughter retire to her bedroom with her when we arrived home.

After supper while doing laundry, I pulled Keely's sweater from the dryer and she immediately ran over and grabbed it out of my hand. Thao's card fell out of the pocket onto the floor. I called Thao to come and get it then Keely slapped me in the face and ran to her room. That really hurt and my cheek turned red but I stiffened up and didn't cry – Thao had his card back. Mother saw the whole thing and later that night she and my father had a loud argument – she wanted to move out! Father was afraid to do so, he had no job, his English was poor, and we couldn't get aid from the government. It seemed hopeless, but mother insisted that we move.

For a week mother searched the area for housing, then she found a duplex in a Vietnamese newspaper. It was located on Lexington Street near my school and this was a pretty nice neighborhood. Rent was only six hundred dollars a month so mother started to look for a job. Again, the newspaper was a big help, they were looking for seamstresses at the clothing factory. They would pay one dollar for every shirt produced. My mother figured that we could get by if she could complete one thousand shirts a month. However, she was hired with the stipulation that she provide the sewing machine. Now, how to pay for this – she took her last piece of gold, a bracelet that her father Nhan had given her and sold it for five hundred dollars. That was enough, she purchased the machine.

As soon as we could, we moved out. I don't know where the first month's rent came from but we were gone from there in three days. Kym was furious! She threatened to call the social services to have us arrested and deported back to Vietnam. My father was afraid of her threat because of his past experiences but mother could have cared less – she did what she had to do! One wonders why Kym reacted that way, she didn't like us there but maybe she was getting some kind of stipend for supporting us.

Our new home was a two bedroom frame house on the corner of the street. Duyen and I had one room and my parents had the other room. My father extended the back of the house into another room for Thao and Phuc, hopefully with the landlord's approval. Aunt Nga moved to San Diego to live with Aunt Thu Hoa and her family. All of us were given our chores while mother spent most of her time sewing shirts. Dad decided to enroll in school to learn more English.

When our first Autumn arrived, it seemed really cold. Of course we didn't have clothes for cold weather, mother hardly had enough money to get us through each month. What I used to do was put my clothes under the sheets and blanket so that they would be warm in the morning. I remember the first time Mrs. Fishbach invited me to her house that Fall for the weekend. Mother planned to let me go so I was excited to leave the family for a weekend excursion.

My duties at home now carried more responsibility – I had to take care of Duyen after school, clean the house, and help with dinner so mother could spend more time on her work. After Duyen went to sleep, I did my homework, sometimes until midnight. My brother Thao helped around the house as much as he could, he was in high school then and he held a part time job to help out the family. My father began to make new friends and he renewed friendships with some of the refugee camp crowd. Unfortunately, he would spend too much time with them hanging out and being idle. I think he was confused and looking for some direction in his life. The language barrier and lack of a trade seemed to bother him.

It soon became time for my weekend visit with Mrs. Fishbach. She drove up that Saturday in a cream colored Volvo sedan. Hien was in the back seat smiling at me as I waved goodbye to mother and dashed to the car. I had to leave without Duyen seeing me or she would have a fit. She was so attached, always next to me whether I was with friends or at a gathering. Hien and I deliberately avoided speaking Vietnamese around Mrs. Fishbach, so we talked in English as she drove along the coast of Huntington Beach. We could see the surfers sitting on their boards in the water patiently waiting to catch a wave. All along the boulevard there were palm trees on each side, accenting the features of the large Spanish style vacation homes.

Soon Mrs. Fishbach announced that we had arrived. She owned a three story beach front town house and it was beautiful. The first floor was the bedroom while the kitchen, living room, and sun room were on the second floor. The third floor was a large open patio filled with exotic plants and a huge parrot. I wondered if he could learn Vietnamese. We loved everything, even the smell of the ocean.

She made us feel at home with peanuts and fruit while we talked for the longest time. Then Hien and I took a walk on the beach and got our feet wet in the cold Pacific water. I enjoyed writing in the sand and then watching the waves come up and erase everything. And all those little sand crabs that would run down the beach toward the water when the wave receded, then run back up the beach in front of the next wave. It was so funny!

There was a stone pier that we just had to walk out on and we went all the way to the end where there was a light pole. We left our names on the pole as a permanent reminder of our visit. About that time our host called us in for lunch, it was a delicious turkey sandwich but different from my usual diet. We could tell that Mrs. Fishbach cared for us as if we were her daughters. She read us a story that night and tucked us into bed. We noticed that she seemed so kind but her pretty face had wrinkles along the eyes and a hint of sadness. When she left the room we started to jabber in Vietnamese well into the night.

On the way home the next day, Mrs. Fishbach invited us to visit her more often, in fact, every other weekend. We agreed after hearing that her daughter lived in New York and her husband was there on extended business. She seemed to be very lonely by herself and we had had a great time so that settled it.

Back home was another matter, mom was throwing dishes on the floor and screaming at my father. It was a real fight, an altercation to be polite. I quickly took Phuc and Duyen to the neighbor's house until the yelling stopped. We played with the other kids and then went back home two hours later when it quieted down. My father had fallen asleep, he had been drunk as usual lately, his way of escaping reality.

I swept up the broken dishes and started to make dinner while wondering where mother had gone. She came home later and had a serious discussion with us. We all sat down while she told us that she was pregnant. We were thrilled at the news but she wasn't ready to accept it under the circumstances. She did promise us though that she wouldn't have an abortion. Life was too precious.

It was really getting cold now, October was about over and Halloween was around the corner. We had heard a lot about the holiday and I couldn't wait to get a costume and collect all those candies. My dear mom took us to the Target store to look for costumes but they were so scary we didn't buy any. Instead, we looked around and then went home to make our own. I found an old black sheet, cut it up, and sewed it into a black Ninja costume for Phuc on mother's sewing machine. For me, I tried on some old clothes and made my face dirty to look like a beggar – that was good enough.

When mother saw me sewing on the machine, she said that I could really help her with her work. My stitching had so improved that she felt that I could assume part of her tasks when she made shirts. Oh well, just another job for me.

Halloween night was extra cold and the sunsets were occurring much earlier so by the time we got started it was already getting dark. The neighborhood kids had already started their rounds with fancy costumes and bags for goodies. They looked so cool but we looked good too. I would say "trick or treat" hoping that we would get a treat because I had no idea what "trick" meant. We finished the neighborhood about eight o'clock and went home to have a feast and to trade some of the goodies. Mother had another idea – she took most of it and put it away so that we wouldn't get sick. For the next year we planned to have better costumes so that we could get more goodies but what we collected now was enough to last a long time – especially with mother in control.

Believe it or not, mother had actually saved enough money, two thousand dollars, to buy father a 1985 Buick sedan. He quickly passed the drivers test so that he could go out with his friends. Meanwhile, mother was getting big in her late term and she was having trouble getting around. I took charge of the cooking and cleaning while Thao would travel the two miles to the Laundromat. He also helped with little Phuc.

The holidays soon rolled around and mother went to the market and purchased a twenty pound turkey for Thanksgiving. We were not sure how to cook the big bird so dad marinated it like the way they used to do when they roasted a duck. This was our first Thanksgiving and a happy one. The Christmas season soon followed and we decided to celebrate the tradition. My mother took us to Home Depot to look for a Christmas tree and we found a five foot beauty with a nice fresh pine smell. We decorated it with cereal and then made ornaments out of tooth picks and beads. It all sparkled from the multi-colored lights that dad had put on the tree. Mom even put presents under the tree with the admonition that they not be opened until Christmas Day.

On Christmas morning the cold weather had put a coating of frost on the windows to add to the ambience. After breakfast we gathered in the living room around the tree and exchanged presents. It was a new and different custom and we really didn't understand the meaning of Christmas but we enjoyed the holiday out of respect for our new surroundings and the people of this great country. And we also thought about the American troops that just left five days ago to invade Panama and catch that drug dealing dictator Noriega and save the Carter treaty that was going to turn over the Canal to them in ten years.

Our religion was still Ong Ba with its connections to Buddhism but mother was so busy trying to make a living that we couldn't attend the temples located along the highway that led to the Vietnamese community. Be that as it may, the appropriate Buddha quote that applied to our situation was very simple – "Work out your own salvation, do not depend on others".

January 15, 1990

This is a date that will be remembered in infamy. My father went out with his friends and got terribly drunk. He insisted on driving home and consequently had a car accident. The car was totaled, not a chance to be repaired and dad was in the hospital for five days. Mother was extremely upset, this was our transportation for work and school. And now that she was seven months pregnant, she couldn't continue to work.

There was no alternative but to visit the social services and apply for Medicaid and welfare. Unfortunately, mother was not approved for welfare. She did get Medicaid coverage for us and the new baby.

A short time later, we happened to meet mother as we were coming home from school. A neighbor had given her an old bike and she told us that she wanted to go to the grocery store. But it was bitter cold and threatening to rain. She went anyway, riding the bike in her condition. How she made it - I still don't know, but she bought six bags of groceries. But in the process the bike had gotten a flat tire. What could she do? She had to balance the packages on the bike and walk along side it carefully so as to not lose any of the bags. Along the way a van pulled up with a big Catholic Church sign on the side. They pulled over and asked mother if she needed any help. The rain had started and was pouring down. She said that she did, then the men asked her if she was Catholic – she said "No". They drove off! Well, that put the frosting on the cake. Not only were we second class citizens under Diem's Catholic regime, we were being discriminated against here! Mother said that we must never marry a Catholic or join the religion – if we did, she would disown us!!

When March arrived mother was about to have the baby. We watched her closely until she started to have frequent pains and our good neighbors were then kind enough to take her to the hospital. My father stayed with mom while Thao stayed in charge of the house to monitor homework lessons and chores that we were assigned. Two days later, mother and her baby boy returned home. He was given the Vietnamese name Diep and we called him Bibi at home. However, his birth certificate had the American name Kevin, a suggestion that Aunt Kym had made when we were on good terms. Before long everyone was settled in including our new family member with his white cheeks and solid black hair.

Mother rested for two weeks and then she began to get better. This was her fifth child at age thirty-six and the strain had shown - what with her stress during the pregnancy. She soon decided that it would be necessary to increase her income, there was another mouth to feed and father still avoided the responsibility of finding a job. He did take care of the baby and helped mother with her sewing while we were at school. His friends were not visiting us anymore since his car accident and that was good, he wasn't drinking as much.

With father now helping mother sew shirts, their income increased enough to purchase a 1988 white Toyota Camry. And dad didn't drive to his friend's house as much, rarely if at all. He seemed more interested in the family yet his poor English skills prevented him from helping with homework – we were left to ourselves on that one.

My mother had so much energy - now she had become a night janitor for a business office. Thao and I would go with her to clean tables and windows, vacuum the floors, and empty the trash cans. We did all right for about two months, good cash money. But then she got fired after some employees saw us helping mother. Their complaint was that child labor laws were being broken. From our point of view, we were just helping out so she wouldn't have to stay out all night. The job required that she go to three offices, twenty miles apart. The loss of the job certainly upset mother but she would think of something else.

Summertime and the living is easy, usually. I liked school so much that I signed up for summer school. I made new friends there, mostly Vietnamese. Walking to school with my girlfriend would have been nice but my parents were afraid that a bully might pick on me or some street gangsters might get me to join them. So walking or the school bus were not an option, dad drove me and my friend every day.

September would begin a new adventure. I was starting Orangeview

Junior High. It was different now, all the kids were big and tall while I was still skinny and petite. That made it tough – I got teased all the time about my appearance and my clothing. They made fun of my accent and told me to go back to my old country. Good old mother reacted and went to a flea market to buy fabric for a dress and skirt that I could wear to school. Thao was also always so considerate, he earned enough money to buy me a very nice sweater at a department store. That sure beat Goodwill. It was kind of big but I liked it and wore it a lot – but only to school. That was fine, I'm very busy at home with Duyen and Kevin.

I liked the idea of the flea market and looked forward to Sundays when my parents would take me with them. There were all kinds of toys and with my allowance for helping to clean, I had saved a few dollars. With this money I bought doll houses and used Barbie dolls for my sister and brother. At home it was fun making miniature furniture and clothes for Barbie. Every night after Kevin was asleep, I would get out the toys and play with Duyen and Phuc. After all, family meant everything to me especially after what we've been through.

I managed to cope with the bullies through the winter. After a while they seemed to let up, but not entirely. My new country was now going through another crisis of its own. It was January and President George H.W. Bush had started Operation Desert Storm to deal with another bully. Saddam Hussein of Iraq had invaded Kuwait and was threatening Saudi Arabia. I had hoped it wouldn't be another Vietnam but this time there were thirty-four countries in the coalition to free Kuwait. It would be a great victory and I was proud of America – it gave me courage to fight my battles!

CHAPTER 9

FORT MYERS

"A New Life"

Wow! My first day of high school at Western High. I was excited to be there but also very nervous. All of the students were big and tall while I was still petite, skinny, dark, and four foot eleven. Like before, they picked on me by making fun of my size and appearance. But worst of all, they would say that I was a waste of space in this country. It made me feel inadequate.

I was so mad when I got home that my mother decided to enroll me into a martial arts class. Our neighbor friend Trang, told us of a recently arrived cousin from Vietnam who had a black belt in Kung Fu. When mother heard of this news, she contacted him and asked if an evening course could be given to the neighborhood children. He agreed and father cleaned out the backyard to make a place to practice and hold classes. The sessions would start at six o'clock and be held for two hours. There were a few boys and girls from the neighborhood that joined up with me.

I learned very quickly because I had an incentive to be the best. That would equalize me with the bullies. A whole range of instruction was given including swordsmanship and stick fighting. This ancient defensive art addressed the internal and external sides of the person and that included conditioning and meditation as well as combat. The practice would improve your mental well being also by bringing emotions and wisdom into harmony. It was called "martial morality". We would even spar with one another and I got beat up a good bit, but I didn't mind – I was becoming skilled!

I didn't say anything at school about my lessons, I just ignored the taunts until one day I went to the gym to change for Phys Ed class. Some of the boys began to make fun of me and then they started to talk nasty about my mother. "Don't say that!" I shouted. That made it worse, they crowded around me and continued to shout in my ear. All of them were six feet tall so I waited for my chance. We passed the teacher's office and approached the pool. I spun around, shouted an animal cry, and jumped up with a kick in the chest of the closest bully. He fell over backward at the edge of the pool and almost rolled into the water.

"Who's next?" I said while looking all of them in the eye. One of my girl friends then yelled out, "Teacher's coming!" We kept on walking, not looking around, and went to class.

After that fight, I waited for the right moment to speak to the bullies. "I'm going to give you guys some more if you piss me off again!" They said nothing, in fact, the boy that I kicked moved away. Once mother heard of this scene, she became afraid that I might get into trouble in the future, so I had to quit taking Kung Fu. But boy – did I ever feel good!!

When it comes to health issues, our culture can be drastically different from American health care. Once when Phuc was sick my mother took a quarter and scraped it across his back and shoulders to drain the pores, then rubbed peppermint on the skin. Of course his back turned red and the neighbors noticed it while he was outside playing. Well, right away they assumed that he was being abused so they called social services and complained about child abuse. The very next day the authorities came to our house and threatened to arrest my parents. They explained to the social workers that the treatment was part of our tradition, there was no abuse. Of course discipline and an occasional spanking would be normal but never to the extreme as surmised by the neighbors. We were monitored for a week and that convinced the case workers that my parents were raising us properly. Interestingly enough, during Christmas time the social services sent us a lot of presents, we got three apiece!

Time quickly passed and Thao graduated from high school. Mother and father bought him a car and gave him a big party. He planned to start college and take a night job to help meet the costs which he didn't want his parents to have to bear. I was about to start my senior year so I asked for permission to find a job as well. Thao's girlfriend and I did find employment at the local shoe store for the weekends. That kept me pretty busy what with school, cooking and cleaning, and caring for my little brothers and sister. They were always glad to be with me during the little time that I had to spare.

When they started Pre-kindergarten I usually went to the teacher conferences and awards programs, just about any school event because mom was constantly working and dad couldn't speak English. So I represented them and was occasionally mistaken for being their young mother. I let them think what they wanted, it was kind of humorous.

In spite of the responsibility that I had shown, my parents became more restrictive as I got older, I couldn't have boyfriends or talk on the phone after 8 o'clock in the evening. And I couldn't wear makeup or lipstick. I was required to concentrate on school and do my chores. Once I put on lip gloss and my mother got furious.

Mother even tried to teach me about sex. But sex is sacred in our culture and she didn't know how to approach the subject. So she purchased an ox organ, brought it home and slammed it down on the wood cutting board to impress me. I jerked back when I heard the loud noise and looked at her. She shocked me when she said,

"This is what an American penis looks like, it is long and big so stay away from it. Also, kisses will make you pregnant."

I laughed to myself and smiled at her. Our health classes in high school covered all aspects of sex and the body but mother didn't know that. It was a strange conversation but I enjoyed talking to mother and getting some attention for a change.

Once again summer arrived and mother, in her usual industrious spirit, discovered a flea market. It was a nice opportunity for a small business. She rented a space on the local parking lot and went into Los Angeles to buy tools, mostly from China. Every weekend dad worked out there selling all kinds of tools; hammers, nails, saws, gloves, power tools and all kinds of hardware items. Early on Saturday morning Thao and Phuc would help father put up the tent and display the tools, then they would go home and back to bed. Mother would bring lunches and give father a break for awhile.

I got a summer job, it was different from the shoe store, I worked the night shift at the local movie theatre. After a while, Mother got tired of carrying me there at 6 pm and returning to pick me up at 2 am. So she insisted that I learn how to drive, after all, I was eighteen years old. I hated the thought of driving in California, the laws are very strict and the people drive like crazy. Mother kept pushing me to get my license though. I hate to admit it, but I failed the test five times, then finally passed it with a barely passing grade. Now that I was driving, I started to save money to buy my own car.

My senior year at last. I got involved in a lot of activities, in particular the Asian club. This club gave me the opportunity to teach a fan dance and a dragon dance. When International Day came around, all of the different clubs entered a dance contest with a dance from each culture. I spent two hours after school every day teaching twelve girls the fan dance. We did quite well against the other groups. Mother, once again, wasn't happy with my extra-curricular activities away from home, so I made sure that I got home early for the rest of the year. When Prom night arrived, I wasn't allowed to go because mother didn't want me staying out late with the boys, I might have gotten raped. No matter, I didn't have a boyfriend anyway.

Thao decided to join the Navy and my parents were devastated. They wanted the children to stay with them forever. But they soon realized that their possessive attitude was wrong. I sensed this right away, mother was more attentive and less strict. Both mom and dad attended my graduation, they didn't give me a party but that was fine – I had graduated!

In fact, two weeks later, I celebrated by taking my three thousand dollars to the car dealer. I bought a new Toyota Corolla. My payments were two hundred and fifty dollars a month with insurance costing another two hundred dollars a month.

I enrolled at the Community College and went there for three years, majoring in Fashion Design. To raise money, I continued working on weekends at the theatre and picked up a few afternoons at the shoe store. It brought in a thousand dollars each month so after my expenses, I gave the rest to my mother.

After that tenure, I received a letter to attend Fashion School. They wanted me to enroll for the next semester but that required that I stay on campus. Mother was angry because Thao had left for the Navy and she still wanted help with the family. After thinking about it for three days, I called the college and declined the offer. That made me feel bad but I got over it and resumed responsibilities for the family.

Our family life seemed to settle down and become more stable after my parents reunited with a lot of our relatives. Two years passed by pleasantly and the family gatherings began to be focused on camping trips. I wasn't too excited about camping but when ten families with at least two children in each decided to get together, it had to be fun. Everyone would bring their own tent and cooking equipment and head for Big Bear Lake in the San Bernardino Mountains. That wasn't too far from Los Angeles in Southern California, just a couple of hours drive.

The scenery was magnificent! The man made Big Bear Lake is surrounded by pine covered mountains and our camp site was at Big Bear Mountain. There was something for everyone – camping, swimming, fishing, hiking, and boating. The clear blue sky gave the fresh water lake a rich blue luster that was framed by the green foliage of the mountains. At night, the surrounding darkness was accented by the thousands of bright stars and the occasional sound of an animal cry. It was beautiful to behold and we enjoyed it while sitting around the campfire roasting marshmallows and drinking cocoa.

I fell in love with the place after the first night but the second night lived up to the campground name. Around two o'clock in the morning I heard heavy breathing. I quietly woke up my sister and slightly opened the zipper to the tent flap. Oh my, there was a huge black bear looking around our camp for food. We were frightened while the bear trashed all of the coolers and then left with a trail of debris behind. Everyone then came outside and admitted that they had been pretty quiet during his visit.

Spring, 1998

Our camping trips now included new friends that mother had made and they enjoyed the gatherings. It was now a family tradition to plan for the camping trips but I didn't like the invitations that mother extended to people that I didn't know. Some of the men would have their eye on me and even suggest that an arranged marriage should be made. Father thought it was a good idea but I hated it. I just turned twenty-one so I argued with my parents a lot about their schemes. After all, I was my own person now and I would decide who I married.

They felt that a marriage to a Vietnamese man of the same culture would be more stable than a marriage with an American. American families divorced all the time and they didn't believe in divorce. So they kept setting up these arranged meetings with Vietnamese men. I wasn't impressed, most of them were drinkers or smokers.

My close friends were aware of these encounters so they set me up with a blind date with a Caucasian. He was tall and kind of cute but I wasn't interested. On the other hand, he was very polite, always a gentleman, and he constantly displayed good manners. So I continued to date him without my parents becoming aware, I would make excuses about my whereabouts. I was actually afraid to introduce him to them.

In the meantime, they kept trying to fix me up with Vietnamese men and I kept refusing to go out with them. It came to a climax when I finally told them that I was dating someone and that he was a Caucasian. They exploded – mother slapped me as hard as she could and threatened to throw me out of the house. I mentioned this to my boyfriend and he asked me to move in with him. I accepted and the day I moved out my little sister cried so much, she was afraid that she would never see me again. Mother refused to talk to me and then threw my clothes out the door. I tearfully left the house and was especially sad for my sister. Mother did make one comment, that I wasn't her daughter. But this was a turning point for me, I didn't want to be trapped like my mother.

I was hurt and bitter. My mother had worked so hard for my father and had put up with so much contention, and for what, to adhere to the Vietnam culture? She couldn't speak up for herself or make decisions, yet she always had to put everyone else first. She sacrificed her happiness because that was expected of her. Not that what she did was wrong, under other circumstances her sacrifices would have been respected and praised. Even so, I still respected the noble life that she led.

But I wanted to get out of that vicious circle and see how other people lived outside of my own kind. So, I took a deep breath and walked out! Two months later I drummed up enough courage to go back to the house with my boyfriend Chris for a proper introduction. This time I would have an engagement ring on my finger. Mom didn't say anything, she left and went to her room with father. We sat in the living room with my brothers and sister and they took an immediate liking to him. We talked and laughed until my mother walked out and said hello. It made me feel better.

April, 2000

Well, I got married and my parents were completely supportive. They invited three hundred guests, aunts and uncles from as far away as Canada and Australia. I was happy to see everyone come to celebrate the big day. I wore the traditional Ao Dai gown of purplish fuchsia trimmed in royal blue. My crown was a round shaped hat of royal blue with gold peacock prints. Most of the family wore Ao Dais as well out of respect for the tradition. There wasn't a church service, it was held at my parents' residence. The ceremony began when the bridesmaid handed me a tea cup which I in turn gave to my parents as a request for their blessing. When my parents drank the tea, it meant that they approved of my marriage. Then they handed me an envelope as a present. It was considered as a good luck token and usually contained money or jewelry. A sort of dowry as the bride and groom started life together.

That Fall, Phuc started college at the University of California, Davis campus. Two years later Duyen entered the University of California at the San Francisco campus. Both majored in Business. Mother and father realized that the children must make their way in life and become established. So with Thao in the Navy and Phuc and Duyen in college, that left Kevin at home.

It wasn't but a few years later that my father developed cancer of the lung. I made an effort to spend quality time with him on all our camping trips. I had reached a point where I could have a confidential conversation with him. I asked him why was he depressed and dependent on alcohol after arriving in America. He replied that he wanted us to have freedom and a better future but the situation for him was not what he expected from America. He couldn't learn the language, or become accustomed to the food, and the people here had too much freedom. Anything goes, it seemed. He felt lost although he tried to be there for his children. He did admit that he didn't try hard enough to become acclimated to his surroundings but now it was too late.

My father often thanked my mother for tolerating him all those years and for taking care of him and coming to his rescue with grandmother. I'm glad he said that but then I saw him start to lose weight while undergoing those treatments. He lost an awful lot of weight and was sick and nauseous all the time.

Phuc changed his name to Kyle because of the pronunciation and he took over the responsibilities of father's medical treatments, paper work, medicines, and doctor's appointments. Duyen would get her Master's degree at age 22 after earning a lot of scholarships. Kyle finished college in record time and now pays the rent and runs the household at age 25. Behind the scenes he had Duyen's courses and budgets all figured out for her and paid any additional costs that she incurred. He had Kevin involved with the ROTC and now he's in the Army. So Kyle is now the patriarch of the family because father succumbed to cancer in 2008. I had moved to Fort Myers, Florida with my husband for employment opportunities. I did return home as often as I was able to get away from work. But when my father passed, I returned to help with the funeral. We almost decided to dress him in his favorite Hawaiian print shirt and polo shorts but the funeral director thought otherwise. We said our goodbyes to father knowing that he is free and in a better place. The house was now empty, no more laughter or tears, so Kyle and My Lien moved to an apartment to get a fresh start. Mom is still trying to adjust to her new life without father.

Despite all the struggles and differences in life, these experiences gave me a lot to be appreciated. We still have each other and we're standing tall. Our heads are held high and our feet are on the ground. We are free,

free from Communism, free from being a slave to a society that no longer controls us.

I am no longer Asian, I am Asian-American! I can never abandon my culture because I believe in that legacy, but I also believe that I can grow and keep changing for the better. God, as we know Him, watches over us because the Keys to His Kingdom belong to everyone!

_____

_____

The great Vietnamese poet Nguyen Chi Thien epitomized the plight and dreams of the refugees in a short verse about the deep night that was overwhelming, yet believing that the dawn would come. His courage to express himself in poetry that was critical of the regime, resulted in twenty-seven years of imprisonment under the most appalling conditions. He embodied the spirit of the people and served as an example for all of us to never give up!

Chao,
Cungdiem Tang

EPILOGUE

Tang Family
Support Organizations for Vietnamese
Fate of the Boat People
Present Status of Camps
Vietnam Today

Tang Family

- Grandmother Tuyet passed away seven years ago. She is laid to rest in the one acre family plot next to her husband Nhan and her Chinese parents.

-Aunt Thu Hoa and her husband are retired and back in Phu Loc.

-Aunt Thu Huong and Aunt My Lan both stayed behind with Tuyet. But they became quite prosperous. They own two hairdresser salons, two beauty schools, and a bridal shop. One is divorced with two grown children and lives in Phu Loc. The other had an arranged marriage with a Vietnamese man and they live in Oklahoma with one grown child.

-Aunt Nga is in San Diego, her American name is Nina.

My Lien's Children:

Thao is in the Navy

Cungdiem is in Annapolis, Maryland. Her name is Denise.

Phuc is now Kyle. My Lien lives with him. He has a Master's Degree in Business, is pursuing a law degree, and is running for City Council in Orange County, California.

Duyen is now Kiera.

Kevin is in the Army.

The family did not pursue United States citizenship initially upon arrival, but they soon realized that they needed to become citizens in order to apply for Medicaid and scholarships.

Cungdiem was eighteen in 1994 when she contacted a lawyer for information. An application had to be filed with a $275 fee. A booklet was then given to her with a four month time period to prepare for an oral test on History and Government. She passed the test and swore under oath her allegiance to the United States and became a citizen. She took the test in English while her parents studied and tested in Vietnamese. Nga, Thao, and Phuc applied at different times.

Support Organizations for Vietnamese

There are support groups for Vietnamese Americans around the United States. One of the most prominent groups is the Boat People SOS Inc. non-profit organization (BPSOS) with headquarters in Falls Church, Virginia. There are thirteen chapters and affiliates around the nation and one in Penang, Malaysia devoted to civic and political activities. Their mission is to empower, organize, and equip Vietnamese individuals, families, and communities to be self-sufficient. Direct services in the areas of health, family, and emergencies will provide a means to liberty with dignity. In 2008, a former board member Anh "Joseph" Cao, became the first Vietnamese-American to be elected to Congress.

A consortium was founded after hurricane Katrina struck New Orleans. This consisted of the Katrina Aid Today (KAT) recovery program and PPSOS in a combined effort to rebuild houses, bank accounts, and social networks. After KAT, additional programs were implemented to help seniors and working families, such as Road To Independence Through Savings and Education (RISE), Seniors and Trauma Survivors Empowerment Program (STEP), and Health Awareness Program For Immigrants (HAPI).

Internationally, an initiative to abolish human trafficking in Southeast Asia was started by BPSOS, the International Society for Human Rights, the Vietnamese Canadian Federation, and the United States Committee to Protect Vietnamese Workers. It was called CAMSA, the Coalition to Abolish Modern-Day Slavery in Asia.

The Legal Assistance for Vietnamese Asylum Seekers (LAVAS) defends victims of persecution including those still in Vietnam and neighboring countries. BPSOS also works with the International Human Rights Society to maintain a list of dissidents arrested since 2007 when a government crackdown started in Vietnam. BPSOS participates in Congressional hearings on Vietnam.

Their website is http://www.bpsos.org/. There is also an online journal titled "Vietnam Review" written in Vietnamese and focused on Vietnam today.

Fate of the Boat People

According to UNHCR, 840,000 Vietnamese people had arrived in Southeast Asia since 1975. About 755,000 were resettled in the West and 81,000 returned safely to Vietnam. With regard to Malaysia, 255,000 of these peoples were given temporary asylum and cared for by the UNHCR and the Malaysian Red Crescent Society. Of that number, 248,410 were resettled in the West and 9,000 returned to Vietnam. At one time, Malaysia had eight camps for the boat people. As the surge of arrivals stopped and more people had been resettled, the remaining refugees were stationed at Sungai Besi.

Between 1975 and 1987, the Vietnamese democide was 1,040,000 people. The breakdown of this number varies with the sources of information but one account shows the following:

Executions: 100,000

Camp Deaths: 95,000

Forced Labor: 48,000

Democides in Cambodia: 460,000

Democides in Laos: 87,000

Boat People Deaths: 500,000

Another source gave 65,000 executions, 165,000 camp deaths, and 200,000 boat people deaths.

The pirate attacks on the boat people began as early as the first escapes in 1975. By 1981, seventy-five percent of the boats that left Vietnam and landed in Thailand were attacked. The numbers fell to 56 percent by 1983. Racial antagonism between Vietnam and Thailand added to the mistreatment. If the boats survived one attack, a second attack was certain, consistently so. Abductions were mostly female and fewer than half were ever found.

The UNHCR received the Nobel Peace Prize in 1981 for its humanitarian efforts

Present Status of Camps

Pulau Bidong – The last refugees were sent home in 1996. At one time, the small island contained 40,000 people. The island's entire vegetation was nearly wiped out. Now the trees are growing again and the island is recuperating. A few volunteers oversee any visitors today and a few scars remain on the hillsides and surviving trees. A few houses remain that sheltered the boat people but for the most part it is vacant and haunting. Since all of the buildings were made of wood, they are near collapse and the surroundings are overgrown with shrubs and weeds. A visitor can still see a kindergarten with paintings and alphabets on the walls although faded by weather. But recently because of the abundance of flora and fauna, it was decided to turn the island into a maritime research center by the University of Malaysia, Terengganu (UMT)

Sungai Besi – The camp is now the home of the National Defense University of Malaysia. This is a military university to prepare men for commissions in the Army, similar to West Point in the United States. Close by is the Sungai Lembing Tin Mine, the largest in the world with 500 miles of tunnels at a depth of 1500 feet. It was flooded during World War Two to prevent the Japanese from mining tin.

Bataan – The Philippine Refugee Processing Center (PRPC) was cancelled in the late 1980's. The camp was closed and fell into the hands of looters and squatters. The Tang family was in one of the last groups to be housed there. But by the 1990's, the Philippine government refused to let the site be reclaimed by the jungle. Instead, it was transformed into the Bataan Technology Park to be associated with the new technical complex on the nearby former Subic Bay Naval Base.

Vietnam Today

Because of the beautiful mountains, wildlife, scenic beaches, ancient pagodas, colorful people, and history, Vietnam is now a thriving tourist attraction. And by the year 2015, a yearly festival will begin for the newly planted Cherry Blossom trees. There will be 56,000 trees located near Dalat in the Central Highlands.

Economic reforms have resulted in millions of visitors each year. Former citizens or Viet Kieu that fled the north in the 1950's and the south in 1975 are now returning with their western culture changing somewhat the established norms of the country. The media and tourism are also influencing the culture. The younger generation is interested in learning English and wearing western clothing, especially jeans. Since their emancipation by the Communist government, the young women are quite affected.

The country still maintains traditions acquired from the Chinese and is still influenced by French architecture and cuisine. During the oppressive communist years, atheism was promoted but today religious practices are re-emerging with a whole range of faiths from Buddhism, ancestor worship, and Confucianism to Catholicism – as long as they do not interfere with the Communist power. A hard line separation of church and state.

Vietnamese is still the official language and the government is a one party system run by the National Congress that meets every five years. Political dissent is not tolerated although public opinion polls are now considered.

The countryside is renewing itself from the ravages of war and the populace is restoring the historical pagodas and French colonial buildings. In 1986, the government started "Doi Moi", an economic reform program to improve manufacturing, trade, agriculture, and forest restoration. The government released the tight reins on economic controls and permitted the free market to flourish – a sort of "westernized communism".

A big help was the lifting of the United States trade embargo in 1994. The next year, normal relations began and in 1997, Douglas Pete Petersen, a former POW, became the American Ambassador to Vietnam. In 2001, the Vietnam National Assembly approved a trade treaty resulting in 4.5

billion dollars of Vietnamese goods being imported by the United States with four times that amount exported to them, all by 2003.

The former Ho Chi Minh trail that flowed through Laos and Cambodia to reach Central and South Vietnam still exists but now a new major highway, the Ho Chi Minh Highway extends from Hanoi down through all of the major Vietnamese cities to Ho Chi Minh city.

There are still border disputes. China occupies the Paracel Islands that lie between Central Vietnam and Luzon in the South China Sea. Vietnam and Taiwan have claims to the islands. The same thing is true of the Spratly Islands on the same latitude as Ho Chi Minh city. This debate includes China, Malaysia, Philippines, Taiwan, and Vietnam. Agreements have been slowly forthcoming with Vietnam continuing construction in the Spratly Islands. In 2005, the national oil companies of China, Philippines, and Vietnam conducted joint marine seismic studies in the Spratly Islands area.

Young five year old Hung Ba Le left Vietnam as a boat person in 1975 and settled in Northern Virginia. He went on to graduate from the United States Naval Academy and progressed to eventually assume command of a guided missile cruiser, the USS Lawson. In November 2009, he officially returned to Danang with his ship where he was welcomed and given the opportunity to visit members of his family at their ancestral home in nearby Hue – a tribute to the better natures of men and their countries.

CONCLUSION

The cold war between the United States and the former Soviet Union gave impetus to the philosophy of containment of Communism. This prognostic mandate by the United States resulted in a vigilant policy toward all non-Democratic countries, especially those in the throes of political turmoil.

So with this ubiquitous monitoring of world affairs, either through diplomatic or clandestine channels, government positions on foreign relationships would be formulated and placed into action as evidenced by the wars in Korea and Vietnam.

These attempts to contain Communism would result in a permanent adversarial posture between two regions of the same nation if complete victory by either side was not obtained – as witnessed by fifty years of struggle between North and South Korea. Yet a victory by one of the adversaries would result in a homogenous nation with regard to government and the application of law – whether fair and balanced or suppressive.

This latter situation was the condition in Vietnam when victory by the Communists was declared and the application of law under the totalitarian regime became prevalent. Aside from an all encompassing government, the people generally remained divided with an ensuing exodus of the free-thinking citizens as evidenced by the culmination of escape attempts by the Vietnamese boat people when prosecution of the dissenters began to take place.

Radical and despotic regimes have been historically the cause of most wars. The attempts to exert hegemony over weaker nations for the purpose of colonization or the acquisition of resources has been occurring for centuries in Europe and the Far East. Stalin, Hitler, Tojo, Kaiser Wilhelm, and lesser dictators, personify these ulterior struggles for power.

However, in the case of Ho Chi Minh, he believed that socialistic communism was the answer to the persecuted history of his people. Indian, Chinese, Japanese, and French encroachments or occupations had influenced the culture and well being of the Vietnamese people for centuries and they had had enough. It was time to control their own destiny and he was prepared to make the attempt. Ultimate victory and the expulsion of French colonialism was then followed by a divided Vietnam under the Geneva Peace Accords with eventual plans for reunification. But the corrupt South Vietnamese democratic government created the necessity in the view of the North Vietnamese government for immediate unification or at least the excuse for immediate unification.

This movement by Ho Chi Minh was considered by the United States as the extension of Communism and a threat to the free world because of the fear of the domino effect – one country becoming communistic with other countries following suit. The American effort in South Vietnam to preserve the fledgling government eventually was withdrawn due to political dissension in the United States. So Vietnam soon became unified as a Communist country.

The average citizen in Vietnam was well aware of the influence of foreign occupation, more so than the difference between Communism and Democracy. Consequently, many people supported Ho Chi Minh for the restoration of their sovereignty regardless of the political philosophy in the rule of government. Communism was seen as the better choice over foreign intervention.

Hanoi exploited the situation and pursued a vendetta against former South Vietnamese officials and citizens thereby removing the illusion that any system was better than foreign intervention. Former soldiers, affluent citizens, religious, officials, and even local peasants were not immune from imprisonment, expulsion, or confiscation of their homes and property. Coupled with these hardships was the depressed economy that reduced employment and goods and services to the point where the quality of life was reduced to survival by any means.

Rather than embracing their former adversaries as Vietnamese citizens, the Communist government created an atmosphere that forced many of them to consider emigration. And by any means available, whether by local fishing boats or a dangerous trek across open country.

This was the state of affairs for the family in this narrative. They were subject to every privation conceivable to the point where they were willing to risk life and limb to escape. Had they been given amnesty or the opportunity to take an oath of allegiance contingent on maintaining ownership of their business, employment, and worldly goods, in so far as the Communist doctrine could provide, the massive exodus would have been drastically reduced and perhaps avoided entirely. But since that was not the case, the blame has to be on the policies of the Hanoi government at that time and the lack of transparency in the line of command from the central government to local officials.

History has shown that elapsed time will heal the devastation of war. The indomitable spirit of the people will prevail with an eventual renewed quality of life. This is evidenced by the westernization of Communist Vietnam. Their economy is booming, and former adversaries are now trading partners. The suppressed people have new opportunities and freedom. Former emigrants have returned to rebuild their lives in their homeland. Had the politicians on all sides acted as statesmen rather than exponents of their policies – policies established without a thorough knowledge or respect for the culture, histories, and values of their opponents, the futility of war could have been avoided.

BIOGRAPHY

Jack Freeze was raised in Baltimore, educated at Johns Hopkins University and retired as a Fellow Engineer. He served eight years in the Naval Reserve and later as Adjunct Professor at the United States Naval Academy. He has authored an historical fiction novel titled, "They Shall Be Remembered."

Cungdiem was born in Phu Loc,Vietnam and then grew up in southern California where she finished high school and attended community college. She now lives in Annapolis, Maryland where she enjoys spending time with her son and family. She follows her father's advice to keep pursuing her dreams.

SYNOPSIS

This is the story of a young girl's family and their struggle to reach America. It is based on the actual diary of the family that was kept and maintained by Cungdiem as she gathered stories from her parents and relatives and combined them with her own experiences. The narrative begins with a description of the early cultural life of the grandparents and relatives in the Mekong Delta.

When the country is divided between the Communists and the corrupt regime of the South Vietnamese government, the United States becomes involved and the war escalates with collateral damage to the countryside and its inhabitants. When South Vietnam finally capitulates, the family becomes directly affected by the Communist victors with the loss of their home and possessions while one of the daughters is forced into an arranged marriage with a South Vietnamese soldier. Part of the family successfully escapes by boat and the young girl's parents attempt an escape on foot through Cambodia. After their capture and release from a remote prison, they attempt an escape by sea where they suffer storms and pirates. Several forays into refugee camps in Malaysia and the Philippines are made until finally they reach the United States.

The struggles continue with turncoat sponsors and school bullies but the family prevails, becomes educated and successful, and accepts their new country with patriotic fervor – two of the sons join the military.